California Governor's Table

Let's Do Lunch

SOUTHERN CALIFORNIA STYLE

EDITED BY
BETTY BROWN SIMM
MARY JANE BENNETT

FOOD STYLIST
ANDREW SPURGIN

PHOTOGRAPHY
SANDRA SMALL

DESIGN BY
MARC HAWKINS

CONTRIBUTING EDITOR
TONI WOODWARD NICKELL

TEXT BY
BETTY BROWN SIMM

SIMM • BENNETT PUBLISHING

MENUS • RECIPES

Dedicated to
ACHIEVEMENT REWARDS FOR COLLEGE SCIENTISTS FOUNDATION, INC.
and all
ARCS SCHOLARS

Flower field in North County, San Diego

Contents

University of California, San Diego

*L*ET'S DO LUNCH Southern California Style is a cookbook adventure, blending the culinary styles of San Diego hostesses with flavors of the Pacific Rim countries.

San Diego beckons, the Lorelei of Southern California. With its choice climate and relaxed lifestyle, "America's Finest City" welcomes the bold, the brave and the daring who are willing to join the city's pioneer heritage of Mexico, the Orient, American Southwest and California.

Passion for souls, gold and freedom brought missionaries, early settlers and the military over the mountains to the safe harbor of San Diego. Nestled in the palm of mountain ranges on three sides, the city flows down to the Pacific Ocean where the U. S. Navy's presence has been such an important part of our nation's history.

Decades of pioneers have built on a fervor for knowledge. They have challenged the sea and the skies, from Sir Francis Drake's galleon to the America's Cup race; Lindbergh's flight to jumbo jets. Research now replaces the early search for freedom, fortune and land. Whether it's agriculture, aerospace, biomedicine or oceanography, San Diego is on the cutting edge of scientific discoveries.

And caregivers smooth the cuts of progress. San Diego women's groups offer helping hands and hearts to implement physical, emotional and educational programs. Recognizing the need to encourage college students studying the natural sciences, medicine and engineering, the San Diego Chapter of ARCS Foundation, Inc. (Achievement Rewards for College Scientists), a volunteer group of women, dedicates 100% of funds raised to scholarships for academically outstanding students at the University of California, San Diego, and San Diego State University.

San Diego State University

In the midst of research and education, San Diegans take time to play on the beach, watch the whales, golf year-round, climb pine-covered hills and smell the flowers. LET'S DO LUNCH provides joyful settings of color — ranunculas, roses, poinsettias — in this, the flower capital of America.

The exuberance and vitality of the potpourri of San Diego have led to a unique entertaining and culinary style that LET'S DO LUNCH shares with you.

A melting pot of flavors and visual impacts from around the world creates San Diego's cuisine. Daring, yet traditional, casual, yet elegant, LET'S DO LUNCH Southern California Style is a delightful gastronomic journey of recipes surrounded by Pacific Rim ambiance.

Open our cookbook, plan a menu from the secret recipes of talented hostesses, and enjoy San Diego's Southern California style of entertaining.

Ballooning over Del Mar

DOCKSIDE AT AMERICA'S CUP

San Diego Harbor

Menu

Chicken Mushroom Soup
Manhattan Clam Chowder
Roasted Butternut Soup
White Chili Soup
Mixed Greens with Dried Cranberries
Parmesan Soup Sticks
Lemon Cream Cake
Rosé

Recipes

CHICKEN MUSHROOM SOUP

(Serves 6)

1 cup boiling water
1/2 oz. dried porcini mushrooms (Italian)
4 slices bacon, chopped
1 medium onion, chopped
1 large garlic clove, chopped
1/2 tsp. dried thyme, crumbled
1/2 pound mushrooms, chopped
1/4 cup flour
4 cups low-sodium chicken broth or chicken stock
1 cup dry white wine
1 Tbsp. tomato paste
1 bay leaf
1 lb. skinned chicken thighs
1 cup half-and-half
Chopped fresh parsley

Combine 1 cup boiling water and dried mushrooms in small bowl. Let stand until mushrooms are soft, about 30 minutes. Drain mushrooms, reserving soaking liquid. Chop mushrooms.

Sauté bacon in heavy large pot over medium heat until crisp. Spoon off 1 tablespoon fat and discard. Add onion to pot and sauté until soft, about 5 minutes. Add garlic and thyme and stir 1 minute. Add both types of mushrooms and sauté until they begin to brown, about 8 minutes. Add flour and stir 2 minutes. Gradually mix in chicken stock. Add wine, reserved mushroom soaking liquid, tomato paste and bay leaf. Bring soup to simmer, stirring until tomato paste dissolves. Add chicken to soup. Cover pot and simmer soup until chicken is just cooked through, about 20 minutes.

Transfer chicken to plate. Cut chicken meat off bones; cut chicken into 1/2-inch cubes. Return chicken to soup. Add half-and-half. Garnish with parsley.

MANHATTAN CLAM CHOWDER

(Serves 8)

3 slices of bacon
1 quart boiling water
3/4 cup cubed celery, carrots and onion combined
1 cup cubed potatoes
$1\frac{1}{2}$ tsp. salt
1 $14\frac{1}{2}$-oz. can stewed tomatoes
2 10-oz. cans chopped clams
1/2 tsp. thyme
Dash of pepper
3 Tbsp. butter
3 Tbsp. quick-mixing flour

Sauté bacon, then mince. Combine bacon, water, celery, carrots, onion, potatoes and salt in soup pot. Cook 15 minutes. Add tomatoes, clams, thyme and pepper. Melt butter over low heat; mix in flour, stir into soup and simmer 15-30 minutes. (May be frozen.)

"I had to sink my yacht to make the guests go home."
F. Scott Fitzgerald

ROASTED BUTTERNUT SOUP

(Serves 8)

4 butternut squash (6 pounds)
6 Tbsp. butter
2 onions, peeled and chopped (Vidalia, if available)
2 Tbsp. curry powder
2 pippin apples, cored, peeled and chopped
6 cups chicken stock
White pepper and salt to taste
Sour cream (optional)

Bake squash at 350 degrees for 1 hour until soft when pierced. Spoon the cooked squash meat out of the skins into the bowl of a food processor or blender. Set aside and cover. Sauté onions in butter for 10 minutes until translucent. Add curry powder and apples and cook until soft. Combine squash, onions and apples and purée until smooth. Add chicken stock. Blend. Add salt and pepper. Blend. If too thick, thin with half-and-half (optional). Serve hot by heating in microwave or serve cold.

Garnish, if served hot: curried croutons and snipped chives.

Garnish, if served cold: sour cream design, as pictured. Place sour cream in pastry bag with a small tip and make an expanding spiral of sour cream on top of soup. Using a toothpick, connect the spirals into the illustrated design.

WHITE CHILI SOUP

(Serves 8)

1 cup onion, chopped
1 Tbsp. oil
3 cloves garlic, pressed
1 4-oz. can green ortega chilies
1 tsp. oregano
2 tsp. cumin
3 cups great northern beans (prepared)
1/4 cup fresh lime juice
5 cups chicken broth (low-sodium, if canned) *4 cups*
1/2 cup chopped cilantro
1/4 tsp. Tabasco
4 cups cooked, cubed chicken
Salt and pepper to taste
Garnish: 1/2 cup Parmesan cheese, grated; 3 green onions, finely chopped

In a large (4-quart) pot, sauté onion in oil until translucent. Stir in garlic, chilies, oregano, cumin and stir until well-mixed. Add beans, lime juice, broth, cilantro and Tabasco. Simmer uncovered 15 minutes. Add cooked, cubed chicken and cover. Simmer 15 minutes more. Adjust seasonings, salt and pepper to taste. Garnish with Parmesan and green onions.

"An idealist is one who on noticing that a rose smells better than a cabbage, concludes that it will also make a better soup."
  H.L. Mencken

Recipes continue on page 84

PACIFIC VISTA

Bird Rock

Menu

LOBSTER SALAD
FAMOUS TOAST
TIRAMISU
CHAMPAGNE

Recipes

LOBSTER SALAD

(Serves 8)

Arugula
Chicory
Spinach
Red & yellow baby pear tomatoes (1 box each)
2 papayas
8-10 tiny new potatoes, steamed in skins, halved
8 hard-boiled eggs, halved
Chives
8 cooked lobster tails, removed from shells

Fill individual salad plates with mixed greens. Garnish with tomatoes, papaya, potatoes, eggs and chives. Place lobster on top. Pass dressing.

EASY SALAD DRESSING

1/2 medium onion
1/4 cup seasoned rice vinegar
1 tsp. sugar
1 tsp. celery seed
1 tsp. salt
1/2 tsp. pepper
1 tsp. prepared mustard
1/2 cup oil

Use the metal blade in the food processor or use food blender. Cut onion and feed through tube. Purée until almost liquid. Add vinegar, sugar, celery seed, salt, pepper and prepared mustard. Blend and slowly add the oil.

FAMOUS TOAST

Use thin-sliced (#12 blade at deli) pumpernickel bread. Brush melted butter on each slice. Cover heavily with grated Parmesan cheese. Place on cookie sheet. Bake at 200 degrees for 1 1/2 hours until crispy. May be stored in plastic bag for next day. Toast may be frozen in airtight bag.

TIRAMISU

(Serves 12-16)

1 16-oz. package Italian ladyfingers
   (If unavailable, use American
   ladyfingers after toasting 10 minutes
   at 375 degrees. Cool.)

6 large eggs, separated
3/4 cup sugar
2 Tbsp. espresso or strong coffee
4 Tbsp. dark rum
1 pound Mascarpone (cheese)
1/4 cup cocoa
1 8-oz. bar semisweet chocolate
Dipping liquid: 3 cups coffee and 1 Tbsp. dark rum

Prepare Mascarpone mix by combining egg yolks, sugar, 2 Tbsp. espresso, 3 Tbsp. rum into a large mixing bowl. Beat with rotary beater for 2-3 minutes. Add Mascarpone and continue to beat for another 3-5 minutes, until consistency is smooth. Set aside.

Combine egg whites with 1 tsp. sugar and beat until mix forms stiff peaks. Gently fold into Mascarpone mix until well-blended.

Pour additional espresso (approx. 3 cups) and 1 Tbsp. dark rum into a flat bowl. Quickly dip each side of ladyfinger and layer on bottom of glass serving dish (9x13-inch uses approx. 24 ladyfingers per layer). Next add a layer of the Mascarpone mixture. Continue with another layer of ladyfingers, then a layer of Mascarpone mix. Top with cocoa (sifted onto top). Let set at least one hour. Top with shaved chocolate.

This dish can be made a day ahead. Wait to top with shaved chocolate until about 2 hours before serving.

"Happiness: A good bank account, a good cook and a good digestion."
   Jean-Jacques Rousseau

"A good cook is like a sorceress who dispenses happiness."
   Elsa Schiaparelli

TAILGATE PICNIC

San Diego Polo

Menu

Garlic and Tarragon Chicken
Potato Dill Salad
Crudités
Epis Bread
Fruit and Nuts
Date Meringue Pie
Chablis

Recipes

GARLIC AND TARRAGON CHICKEN

(Serves 8)

1/2 cup olive oil
4 large garlic cloves, pressed
4 Tbsp. dried tarragon, crumbled
2 3 1/2-pound chickens, cut into pieces

Preheat oven to 500 degrees. Combine oil, garlic and tarragon in bowl. Coat chicken pieces with oil mix. Arrange chicken on baking sheet. Season to taste with salt and pepper. Bake 10 minutes. Reduce heat to 375 degrees. Bake until chicken is done, about 30 minutes longer.

"The secret to a long life is to stay busy, get plenty of exercise and don't drink too much. Then again, don't drink too little."
  Hermann Smith-Johannson, at age 103

POTATO DILL SALAD

(Serves 8)

8 potatoes
4 hard-boiled eggs
1 cup oil
1/2 cup wine vinegar
1 Tbsp. sugar
1/2 cup sweet pickle relish
1/2 cup chopped onion
1 cup chopped celery
1/4 cup chopped fresh dill
1 tsp. celery seed
Salt and pepper to taste

Boil 8 potatoes and peel while still warm. Dice immediately and add eggs while potatoes are warm. Mix in rest of ingredients. Salt and pepper to taste. Refrigerate. Make one day ahead.

EPIS BREAD

(Makes 2 loaves)

1 1/2 packages active dry yeast
1 Tbsp. sugar
2 cups warm water (100-115 degrees)
1 Tbsp. salt
5-6 cups all-purpose flour
3 Tbsp. yellow cornmeal
1 Tbsp. egg white mixed with 1 Tbsp.
   cold water (egg wash)

Combine yeast with sugar and warm water in a large bowl and allow to set 15 minutes. Mix the salt with flour and add to the yeast mix a cup at a time until there is a stiff dough. Remove to a lightly floured board and knead until no longer sticky (10 minutes), adding flour as necessary. Put into a buttered bowl and turn to coat the surface with butter. Cover and let rise in a warm place until doubled in bulk (1 1/2 to 2 hours). Punch down the dough. Turn out onto a floured board and shape into 2 long loaves. Place on a baking sheet that has been sprinkled with cornmeal, but not buttered. Cut the sides of dough partway, diagonally, about 3 inches apart, alternating so the cuts are not opposite each other (shape of wheat). Brush with egg wash. Place on cookie sheet in cold oven, set the temperature at 400 degrees and bake 35 minutes or until well-browned and hollow sounding when the tops are rapped.

DATE MERINGUE PIE

(Serves 6)

10 soda cracker squares
1 cup white sugar
2 tsp. baking powder
3 egg whites
1 tsp. vanilla
1/2 cup dates
1/2 cup walnuts

Roll crackers. Add sugar and baking powder. Fold all into stiffly beaten egg whites. Fold in vanilla, dates and nuts. Place in buttered 8-inch pie tin. Bake 30 minutes at 350 degrees. Cut in pie-shaped pieces and serve with whipped cream or ice cream.

"Cooking is like love. It should be entered into with abandon or not at all."
   Harriet Van Horne

ITALIAN WINE CELLAR

Fairbanks Ranch

Menu

ANTIPASTI
TRI-COLOR PESTO PASTA WITH FRESH VEGETABLES
FRENCH BREAD DIPPED IN OLIVE OIL
COFFEE TORTONI
CHIANTI

Recipes

ANTIPASTI

Chop tomatoes and garlic with fresh basil, salt and
   pepper, extra virgin olive oil
Black olives
Grissini (little bread sticks) wrapped with Prosciutto
Miniature artichokes with lemon slices
Baked Garlic with Thyme

Baked Garlic with Thyme

8 heads whole garlic
1/4 cup extra virgin olive oil
Salt and pepper
3 tsp. chopped fresh thyme
1/4 cup white wine
8 oz. Roquefort cheese, grated

   Preheat oven to 300 degrees. Remove
some of the loose papery skins from garlic
heads. Slice tops off the whole heads to
expose cut garlic cloves. Arrange heads in
a garlic baker with cut sides up. Drizzle
with olive oil and sprinkle with salt,
pepper and chopped fresh thyme. Pour
over wine. Place lid on baker and bake at
300 degrees for 1 hour. Remove lid and
baste with olive oil and wine in baker.
Bake for another 30 minutes. Add
Roquefort to garlic tops, cover and bake
another 10 minutes. Serve.

TRI-COLOR PASTA

(Serves 10-12)

Golden (basic)

2 cups semolina flour
2 eggs
1 Tbsp. olive oil
2 Tbsp. water

Green: Eliminate water, add 1/4 cup cooked
   spinach, well-drained, puréed
Orange: Eliminate water, add 1/4 cup cooked
   carrots, puréed
Red: Eliminate water, add 1/4 cup puréed beets
   (add 3 Tbsp. vinegar to water when cooking to
   preserve color)
Quick Color: Eliminate water, add 1/4 cup puréed
   baby-food vegetables (spinach, carrots or beets)

   Mound flour on smooth flat surface.
Make a deep well in the center and break
eggs, one at a time, into well, beating
between each addition. Use a fork to beat
eggs lightly, then mix in water and oil.
Beat again. Mix the flour into the well of
liquids with the fork. Use hands to
finish. Mix until stiff. Fold and press the
dough several times, kneading into a ball.
If the dough is sticky, add a little flour; if
crumbly, add a few drops of water. Clean
the surface and flour lightly, then knead
dough until it is smooth, elastic and no
longer sticky (10-15 minutes).
   Cover and let dough rest for 30
minutes. Roll out one-fourth of the
dough at a time on a manual pasta
machine. On each fourth part of dough,

continue rolling until pasta reaches desired thickness (roll about 5 times). Place on rack to dry for 1 hour.

Ribbon Pasta

Colored pasta can be joined after cutting into narrow strips and moistening with water along edge, pressing together and rolling once more. Boil pasta for 4 minutes in 4 quarts water and 1 Tbsp. olive oil.

PESTO WITH FRESH VEGETABLES

(Serves 8)

Vegetables

2 cups thinly sliced mushrooms
3 Tbsp. olive oil or butter
4 medium carrots, cut in 2x1/4-inch julienne
1 pound snow peas, trimmed and cut in 1-inch pieces
1 yellow bell pepper, cut in 2x1/4-inch julienne
8 thin asparagus spears, cut in 2-inch pieces

Pesto

1 cup fresh basil leaves, washed and dried
2 cloves garlic
1 cup pine nuts
1 cup freshly grated Parmesan cheese
1/2 cup freshly grated Romano cheese
1/4 cup olive oil
1/2 cup dry white wine
1/2 cup boiling water

Sauté mushrooms in olive oil or butter until cooked. Set aside. Steam carrots, peas, bell pepper and asparagus until fork-tender, 3-5 minutes. Drain and combine with mushrooms. Set aside. Combine basil, garlic and pine nuts in a blender or food processor and purée until smooth. Add Parmesan and Romano cheeses. Blend. Pour in olive oil and mix. Add wine and mix. Pour in boiling water. Blend. Add more wine if too thick for addition of vegetables. Combine with vegetables in a pot and warm over low heat on stove top or in microwave. Ladle over hot pasta. Garnish with pine nuts and Parmesan.

DIP FOR FRENCH BREAD

1/2 cup olive oil
1 large clove garlic, pressed
1 Tbsp. chopped fresh basil leaves, or
    1/4 tsp. dried basil

Mix all ingredients and place in cruet. To serve, pour on bread & butter plate. Dip bread into oil instead of using butter.

"A man doesn't live by bread alone. He needs buttering up once in a while."
    Robert H. Henry

Recipes continue on page 85

LAKESIDE IN THE GROVES

Poway Hidden Valley

Menu

Brandied Veal
Gnocci or Noodles
Vegetable Collage
Spice Pumpkin Bread
Orange Meringue Lovely
Pinot Noir

Recipes

BRANDIED VEAL

(Serves 8)

3 pounds scallopini veal round

All-purpose flour

2 10-oz. packages frozen artichoke hearts, thawed and cut in half

2 Tbsp. finely chopped shallots

2 lbs. mushrooms, sliced thin

Salt and pepper to taste

1/2 cup brandy

3 cups Brown Sauce Mix or 2 packages Hunter Sauce Mix (prepare per directions)

3/4 cup heavy cream

Place any thick pieces of veal between wax paper sheets and pound with mallet to flatten. Flour veal lightly. Sauté veal in large skillet in butter about 1 minute each side. When veal is light brown, add artichoke hearts, shallots, mushrooms, salt and pepper. Sauté a few minutes. Add brandy and sauté another minute longer, adding butter as needed. Remove veal. Add cream and brown sauce. Cook until sauce is thick and smooth. Return veal to pan and heat thoroughly. Serve over noodles or gnocci.

"Claret is the liquor for boys, port for men; but he who aspires to be a hero must drink brandy."

Samuel Johnson

PARSLIED GNOCCI OR NOODLES

Cook pasta according to directions on the package. Toss with chopped parsley and butter.

VEGETABLE COLLAGE

(Serves 8)

5 zucchini

5 yellow crookneck squash

3 carrots

1 large onion

1 large red bell pepper

4 Tbsp. dried tomato seasoning flakes

Salt and pepper to taste

5-6 Tbsp. water

Slice first 3 ingredients in 1/2-inch slices. Thinly slice onion (leave in rings). Slice bell pepper in 1/4-inch strips. Spray 9x12-inch baking dish with nonstick cooking spray. Toss all vegetables in baking dish. Sprinkle with dried tomato flakes. Add 5-6 Tbsp. water. Cover with plastic wrap. Bake in microwave on High 10 minutes. Salt and pepper to taste.

SPICE PUMPKIN BREAD

(Serves 10)

1 cup oil
3 cups sugar
4 eggs, slightly beaten
2 cups pumpkin (cooked or canned)
2/3 cup water
3 1/3 cups flour
2 tsp. baking soda
1 1/2 tsp. salt
1 tsp. cinnamon
1 tsp. nutmeg
1/2 cup chopped nuts (walnuts or pecans)

Mix oil and sugar. Beat until well-blended. Add eggs. Blend thoroughly until light and fluffy. Add pumpkin and water and blend. Sift flour, soda, salt and spices together. Add to pumpkin mixture. Add nuts. Place in 3 small, or 2 large, greased bread pans. Bake at 350 degrees for 1 hour.

"He that is of a merry heart hath a continual feast."
Proverbs 15:15

ORANGE MERINGUE LOVELY

(Serves 12)

Meringue Shell

6 egg whites
1/2 tsp. cream of tartar
1/4 tsp. salt
1 1/2 cups sugar

Orange Filling

6 egg yolks
3 Tbsp. sugar
1 6-oz. can frozen orange juice, thawed, undiluted
1 Tbsp. grated orange peel
2 cups whipping cream

Beat egg whites until foamy, then add cream of tartar and salt. Beat until stiff, but not dry. Add sugar gradually, beating until stiff. Cover baking sheet with aluminum foil. Spread layer of meringue in 9-inch circle. With a tablespoon, shape puffs around circle to form a wall for filling. Bake at 275 degrees for 1 hour. Cool.

Beat egg yolks, then add sugar and orange juice. Cook over boiling water, stirring constantly. Add grated orange peel. Remove from heat and chill. Whip cream and fold into orange mixture. Spoon into meringue. Cover and chill 12-24 hours.

Individual Orange Lovelies (Serves 6)

Make half recipe for meringue and filling. Prepare meringue and shape into 6 3-inch rounds on aluminum foil. Make a 2-inch hollow in center for filling. Bake as directed. Fill and chill. Garnish with mint sprig.

OHIRO

La Jolla

Menu

STUFFED SHRIMP
CRAB-FILLED CUCUMBERS
MISO-MARINATED ASPARAGUS
SUSHI
STEAMED RICE
GREEN TEA ICE CREAM
RICE WINE OR WHITE RIESLING

Recipes

STUFFED SHRIMP

(Serves 8)

12 large raw shrimp with tails

Marinade

1/2 cup rice vinegar
2/3 cup water
2 tsp. sugar
Salt to taste

Filling

4 hard-boiled egg yolks, finely mashed
2 Tbsp. lemon juice
2 Tbsp. red cocktail sauce
1 tsp. fresh dill leaves, finely chopped

Cook shrimp with shells on. To prevent shrimp from curling when they cook, spear them along their inner curve with toothpicks or small skewers. Place in boiling water, uncovered, for 3 minutes or until pink and still firm. Cool under cold water. Remove toothpicks. Peel shrimp, leaving tail on. Devein, then butterfly shrimp (cut along inner curve, spread open and slightly flatten).

Add shrimp to marinade and set aside. Combine filling ingredients. Drain shrimp. Place 1 Tbsp. filling into each shrimp. Close the two shrimp sections and press firmly. Serve.

CRAB-FILLED CUCUMBERS

(Serves 8)

4 cucumbers
1 bunch watercress
2 pounds crabmeat
1 bottle pickled ginger, shredded

Peel cucumbers and cut lengthwise. Marinate in salt water for 20 minutes. Then wash and dry. With spoon, remove seeds and pulp to make a hollow lengthwise. Wilt leaves of watercress in boiling water for 30 seconds. Run under cold water. Drain and dry. Place half of watercress in hollowed half cucumber, then enough crabmeat pressed together with 1 strip of pickled ginger alongside to fill. Repeat with other half cucumber. Press cucumber halves together. Cut into 1/2-inch rounds. Serve with dipping sauce.

Sambai-Zu Dipping Sauce

2 1/2 Tbsp. rice vinegar
2 1/2 Tbsp. clam juice
4 tsp. sugar
2 tsp. soy sauce

Combine all ingredients.

MISO-MARINATED ASPARAGUS

(Serves 8)

Miso

30-oz. package Shiro Miso (white soybean paste)
1 1/2 cups sugar
1 cup sake (rice wine)
2 egg yolks

Cook, stirring constantly, Shiro Miso, sugar and sake. Bring to boil, then simmer for 30 minutes. Remove pan from heat and beat in egg yolks, one at a time. Dip pan in ice water to cool. If tightly covered, will keep 6 months in refrigerator. Makes 1 quart.

20 asparagus spears
1 cup Miso (soybean powder available prepared in Oriental section of market)
1 tsp. powdered mustard

Slice asparagus in 1/2-inch pieces and drop into boiling water. Boil for 1 minute. Drain and immerse in cold water. Drain and dry. Mix Miso and mustard. Spread half of mixture in dish. Place half of asparagus on top, then remaining mixture and top with remaining asparagus. Marinate for 3 hours. Remove asparagus from marinade and serve.

"Give a man a fish and he will live for a day; give him a net and he will live for a lifetime."
  Chinese Proverb

SUSHI

(Serves 8)

1 cup unconverted white rice
2 pounds raw paper-thin white fish fillets
Toasted sesame seeds

Vinegar Dressing

1/4 cup rice vinegar
3 Tbsp. sugar
2 Tbsp. dry sherry
Salt and pepper to taste

Cook rice according to directions on package. Set aside for 5 minutes. Combine cooked rice with vinegar dressing. Place in pan and bring to a boil. Cool. Place 1 tsp. rice on a slice of fish. Wrap fish and rice in cheesecloth and squeeze into a ball. Remove cheesecloth. Sprinkle fish ball with sesame seeds and serve.

"He was a bold man that first ate an oyster."
  Jonathan Swift

SUPER BOWL BUFFET

Fairbanks Ranch

Menu

BURGUNDY BEEF OR LAMB MOROCCO OR
FISH STEW WITH ROUILLE SAUCE
FENNEL HARVEST
CAESAR SALAD
HERB BREAD
CARROT CAKE
MERLOT

Recipes

BURGUNDY BEEF

(Serves 8)

3 pounds beef stew meat
2 cups coarsely chopped onion
5 cloves garlic, pressed
1 1/2 tsp. each thyme, marjoram and sugar
1 tsp. salt
1 tsp. pepper
2 cups hearty Burgundy
2 12-oz. jars beef or brown gravy
1/3 cup brandy
4 cups mushrooms, cleaned and halved
2 20-oz. bags frozen stewing vegetables, thawed
1 cup sour cream, room temperature (optional)
1 10-oz. box frozen petite peas, thawed

Place meat in ovenproof casserole. Add onion, garlic, seasonings and liquids (except sour cream). Stir. Bake at 300 degrees for 3 hours. Add mushrooms and thawed vegetables, but not peas, and bake 1 hour more. Add sour cream, if desired, and stir. Warm thawed petite peas in microwave 1 minute. Scatter over casserole or individual plates when serving.

LAMB MOROCCO

(Serves 6-8)

3 Tbsp. olive oil
3 pounds boneless lamb shoulder, cut in 2-inch cubes
2 large onions, finely chopped

1 28-oz. can tomatoes, drained
1 cup white vermouth
1 cup beef broth
1 1/2 tsp. cinnamon
1/2 tsp. saffron
1/2 tsp. ginger
1/2 tsp. cardamom
1 cup golden raisins
1/2 cup chopped almonds
Salt and pepper to taste

In heavy casserole, brown lamb in oil in batches. Add onions and cook until golden. Add remaining ingredients, except salt and pepper. Cook gently on top of stove until lamb is tender, about 2 to 3 1/2 hours. Add salt and pepper to taste. Thicken with mix of 1/2 flour to 1/2 cornstarch to desired consistency.

FISH STEW WITH ROUILLE SAUCE

(Serves 8)

Rouille Sauce

2/3 cup mayonnaise
2 cloves garlic
3/4-1 tsp. cayenne
1 Tbsp. white wine vinegar
1/4 tsp. salt

Mix Rouille Sauce, cover and chill.

Continues on top of next page

Fish Stew

2 Tbsp. oil

1 large onion, chopped

1 large green pepper, chopped

2 cloves garlic, chopped

1 16-oz. can pear tomatoes, broken up

1¹/₂ cups water

1/2 cup white wine

8-oz. bottle clam juice

3 cubes chicken bouillon

1/4 tsp. each basil, oregano, thyme

4 pounds clams, scallops, lobster, crab or any mild fish
fillets, cut into 1-inch cubes

In 5-quart kettle, heat oil. Add onion, green pepper, garlic and cook until limp. Add tomatoes, water, wine, clam juice, bouillon cubes, basil, oregano and thyme and simmer 15 minutes. Bring broth to boiling and add fish. Cook 5-10 minutes or until clams open. Top with 1-3 tsp. Rouille Sauce per serving.

FENNEL HARVEST

(Serves 8)

4-6 fennel bulbs (anise), quartered with layers
separated except for heart of bulb

1¹/₂ 24-oz. bags of baby carrots, peeled

8 jumbo mushrooms, cleaned and quartered

3 small zucchini, sliced in 1-inch rounds

Extra virgin olive oil, as needed

Freshly ground pepper

2 10-oz. boxes of couscous (unseasoned)

4 ¹/₂ cups of nonfat, low-sodium chicken or vegetable
stock (can substitute water for part of the stock)

Preheat oven to 425 degrees. Prepare fennel, carrots and mushrooms and place in 2-gallon sealable plastic bag. Prepare zucchini and place in separate small sealable plastic bag. Add olive oil to both bags, just enough to slightly coat vegetables. Close bags and "toss" vegetables in bags to thoroughly coat vegetables with the oil. This preparation can be done 3-4 hours before cooking, with vegetables remaining at room temperature.

To cook: Empty fennel, carrots and mushrooms into large, shallow, ungreased roasting pan, spreading vegetables so they are not too deeply stacked. Roast for 25 minutes, tossing 2-3 times for even browning. Add zucchini and freshly ground pepper, evenly mixing among roasted vegetables. Roast for 10 more minutes.

Bring the stock to a boil in a large saucepan, stir in the couscous, cover and remove from heat. Couscous will be ready in 5 minutes; fluff with fork before serving. Arrange roasted vegetables on top or around the couscous and serve steaming hot.

"At a party one should eat wisely but not too well, and talk well but not too wisely."
    W. Somerset Maugham

Recipes continue on page 85

A TASTE OF SOUTHWEST

Rancho Santa Fe

Menu

Yellow Corn Posole
Achiote Chicken
Spicy Black Beans
Mango and Passion Fruit Salsa
Sliced Fruit
Beer Bread
Flan
Beer

Recipes

YELLOW CORN POSOLE

(Serves 10 or more)

1 1/2 cups fresh white or yellow corn kernels
   (grill, unhusked, beforehand)
1 14-oz. can black-eyed peas, drained
1 15.5-oz. can white hominy, drained
2 medium tomatoes, seeded and chopped
4 green onions, very thinly sliced
2 garlic cloves, peeled and minced
1 medium green bell pepper, finely chopped
   (can grill first)
1/2 cup chopped yellow onion
1/3 cup chopped cilantro
1 cup picante salsa

   Combine all ingredients and mix
lightly. Cover and chill for at least 2 and
up to 24 hours, stirring occasionally.
Drain before serving. Serve with white
corn chips.

*"Part of the secret of success in life is to
eat what you like and let the food fight
it out inside."*
  Mark Twain

ACHIOTE CHICKEN

(Serves 8)

4 boneless, skinless chicken breasts, halved
2 tsp. achiote paste (available in Mexican
   food stores)
1/4 cup extra virgin olive oil
3 garlic cloves, pressed
1 cup fresh squeezed orange juice

   Combine achiote paste and olive oil.
Add pressed garlic cloves. Mix with
orange juice. Place chicken breasts in a
single layer in an ovenproof pan. Pour
orange juice mixture over the chicken.
Bake for 25-30 minutes, or until done, at
350 degrees.
   Instead of baking, barbecue over
mesquite.

SPICY BLACK BEANS

(Serves 4)

1 cup dried black beans
1 Tbsp. peanut oil
1 Tbsp. cumin
1/2 yellow onion, finely chopped
1 whole dried chili
1 Tbsp. chopped garlic
Salt and pepper to taste
Optional: cayenne (to a "fire" level that's comfortable
  to one's taste buds)
Garnish: sour cream, snipped chives, fresh mango
  passion fruit salsa (recipe follows), cilantro or
  shaved asiago cheese

Pick over and wash black beans. Sauté cumin, onion, chili and garlic in peanut oil until onion is soft. Add beans and cover with water, plus two inches extra. Bring to a boil and reduce to simmer. Cook 1 to 1 1/2 hours, or until beans are tender. Add water, if necessary. Do not let the beans go dry. Add cayenne, if desired.

Garnish, as desired, with ingredients listed above, and serve.

BEER BREAD

(Serves 6)

3 cups sifted self-rising flour
2 Tbsp. sugar
12 oz. beer

Mix together; don't beat. Put into greased 8x4-inch loaf pan. Let set 1/2 hour. Bake 1 1/4 hours at 350 degrees.

MANGO AND PASSION FRUIT SALSA

(Serves 6)

1 Tbsp. peanut oil
1 small yellow onion, diced
1 jumbo garlic clove, or 2 small cloves, pressed
2 slightly underripe mangoes, diced medium
2 passion fruits, juice and pulp only
1 jalapeño pepper, seeded, deveined and diced
1/3 cup chopped cilantro
1 lime, juice and zest
1 lemon, juice and zest
1 red bell pepper, seeded, deveined and diced

Toss the onion and garlic clove in peanut oil. Place in pan and roast at 350 degrees until slightly brown. Mix all remaining ingredients together in order; set aside to top black beans.

FLAN

(Serves 6)

2 cups dry sherry
1/2 cup superfine granulated sugar
1/8 tsp. cinnamon
6 egg yolks

In a saucepan, combine sherry, sugar and cinnamon. Bring mixture slowly to a boil. Beat egg yolks until foamy and mix with a little hot wine mixture. Slowly stir yolks into wine mixture and strain into custard cups. Set in pan of hot water. Bake at 350 degrees for 45 minutes. Chill and serve very cold.

BUTTERFLY CONNECTION

Wild Animal Park

36

Menu

SHRIMP BISQUE
SURPRISE GREEN SALAD
HONEY-MUSTARD PORK
ORANGE PRALINE YAMS
ZUCCHINI BREAD
FRUIT PIE
WHITE SANGRIA

Recipes

SHRIMP BISQUE

(Serves 8)

1 ½ pounds cooked shrimp
6 Tbsp. butter
2 Tbsp. onion
3 cups warm milk
1 cup cream
1/2 tsp. salt
1/4 tsp. white pepper
1/4 tsp. nutmeg
3 Tbsp. sherry
2 Tbsp. chives

Shell and clean shrimp. Place in food processor with blade for chopping. Process until no longer lumpy. Place butter and onion in top of double boiler and cook over boiling water for 5 minutes. Add the ground shrimp and warm milk. Cook for 2 minutes. Stir the cream in slowly and add the seasonings, sherry and chives. Stir. Serve with crackers.

SURPRISE GREEN SALAD

(Serves 6)

1 head romaine
1 garlic clove, halved
2-3 Tbsp. extra virgin olive oil
4 slices bacon, diced and sautéed
Tomato wedges
Avocado wedges
Salt

Mint leaves, minced
1 egg
1/2 lemon
Dried oregano
Freshly grated Parmesan cheese

Place olive oil in wooden salad bowl with salt. Rub bowl with cut faces of garlic, using salt as abrasive. Let clove sit in bowl while preparing the rest. Sauté bacon and drain. Discard garlic and place tomato and avocado in bowl, adding torn (or cut, if done at last minute) romaine. Mix egg with juice of 1/2 lemon in small bowl and add. Sprinkle bacon, mint and oregano over top to taste. Grate fresh Parmesan liberally over salad. Toss at last minute and serve. Croutons and green onions may be added, if desired. Taste salad, adding more lemon juice and oil, if needed.

HONEY-MUSTARD PORK

(Serves 8)

1 ½ cups beer
1 cup Dijon mustard
1/4 cup honey
1/2 cup olive oil
4 Tbsp. chopped fresh rosemary (or 2 Tbsp. dried)
4 Tbsp. chopped garlic
4-pound boneless pork loin roast
1 cup cream
Salt and pepper to taste

Continues on top of next page

Whisk first 6 ingredients to blend in 8x8x2-inch glass baking dish. Add pork and turn to coat. Let stand at room temperature 1 hour.

Preheat oven to 350 degrees. Transfer pork to rack set in roasting pan; reserve marinade. Roast until thermometer inserted into center registers 150 degrees. Let stand 15 minutes.

Strain marinade into heavy medium saucepan. Add cream and juices from roasting pan. Boil sauce until reduced to 3 cups, about 15 minutes. Season with salt and pepper.

Slice pork; arrange on warm platter. Drizzle some sauce over. Serve, passing extra sauce separately.

ORANGE PRALINE YAMS

(Serves 8-10)

5 pounds canned yams, drained
2/3 cup orange juice
1 Tbsp. grated orange rind
5 Tbsp. brandy
2 tsp. salt
Pepper to taste
1 tsp. ground ginger
1/4 cup butter
1/3 cup light or golden brown sugar, packed
3 egg yolks

Praline Topping

2/3 cup light or golden brown sugar, packed
1 cup chopped pecans (about 4 oz.)
1/4 cup butter, melted
1 tsp. ground cinnamon

Beat yams until smooth. Mix in remaining yam ingredients until mixture is light and fluffy. Butter 12-inch porcelain quiche dish or shallow 2-quart casserole (7x11-inch) and add yam mixture in smoothing evenly. Mix praline ingredients in bowl and spread over yams. May be refrigerated overnight.

Bake at 350 degrees for 45-50 minutes or until golden brown and bubbly. Let stand 10 minutes before serving.

ZUCCHINI BREAD

(Makes 2 loaves)

3 eggs
2 cups sugar
3 tsp. vanilla
1 cup oil
2 cups grated zucchini
3 cups flour
1/4 tsp. baking powder
1 tsp. salt
1 tsp. baking soda
3 tsp. cinnamon
1 cup chopped nuts (walnuts)

Beat eggs. Add sugar, vanilla and oil. Blend well. Stir in grated zucchini. Sift flour, baking powder, salt, baking soda and cinnamon. Blend with creamed mixture. Fold in chopped nuts. Turn into two greased and floured 9x5-inch loaf pans. Bake at 350 degrees for 1 hour.

Recipes continue on page 86

AFTER THE HUNT

Cedar Hills Farm

Menu

Marinated Quail
Minted New Potatoes
Pink Beauty
Sautéed Portobello Mushrooms
California Crêpes
Fresh Strawberries
Sherry or Claret Cup or Mint Julep

Recipes

MARINATED QUAIL

(Serves 4)

8 quail (domestic)
2/3 cup dry white wine
3 Tbsp. lemon juice
3 bay leaves, crushed
1/4 cup chopped onion
6 peppercorns, crushed
1/2 tsp. dried rosemary, or 1 1/2 tsp.
   fresh rosemary, chopped
2-3 Tbsp. butter, melted
Salt and pepper to taste

Clean and butterfly the quail; place in a shallow pan. Combine wine, lemon juice, bay leaves, onion, peppercorns and rosemary. Pour over quail and marinate for 2 hours. Remove birds from pan and place in broiler pan. Dry and brush with melted butter. Place 4 inches from broiler and cook 5 minutes on a side. Salt and pepper to taste. Serve hot with fresh rosemary garnish.

MINTED NEW POTATOES

(Serves 4)

12 small new potatoes
2 Tbsp. butter
Salt and pepper
Fresh mint

Steam potatoes until cooked. Cut in half, unless tiny. Toss with melted butter and chopped fresh mint. Salt and pepper to taste. Serve.

PINK BEAUTY

(Serves 4)

1 small head red cabbage
1 small onion, chopped
2 tsp. salt
1/2 cup vegetable oil
3/4 cup sugar
3/4 cup white vinegar

Shred cabbage and place in heat-resistant glass bowl. Mix with chopped onion and salt. Combine vegetable oil, sugar and white vinegar in saucepan. Bring to a boil and pour over the cabbage. Do not mix. Cool and cover. Refrigerate overnight. Serve in bowl.

"The discovery of a new dish does more for human happiness than the discovery of a new star."
   Anthelme Brillat-Savarin

SAUTÉED PORTOBELLO MUSHROOMS

(Serves 4)

2 large Portobello mushrooms
1 Tbsp. butter or olive oil
Garnish: parsley and lemon

Use a moistened mushroom brush to clean the mushrooms. Don't let the underside get wet. Pat dry. Sauté mushrooms on low heat capside down in butter or oil for 15 minutes, adding oil to pan, if needed. Place on serving plate capside up. Garnish with parsley and lemon. Cut in wedges and serve.

CALIFORNIA CRÊPES

(Makes 12 crêpes)

1 cup flour
1/2 tsp. salt
1 Tbsp. sugar
1 tsp. baking powder
4 eggs
1 1/2 cups milk
Butter

Mix flour, salt, sugar and baking powder and sift into bowl. Set aside. Break eggs into a large bowl and beat until frothy. Add milk and blend. Resift flour mixture, a little at a time, into egg mixture, while beating.

Place a pancake/omelet skillet over medium heat and add 1 Tbsp. butter. When melted, place 1/4 cup crêpe batter into skillet and tilt pan until batter covers bottom. Cook until bubbles form at edges (about 1 minute). Turn crêpe with spatula and cook on second side for 1 minute. Crêpes may be rolled and kept warm in 250-degree oven while others are cooked. Serve.

Options:

To use as main dish, fill crêpes with chicken or crab Mornay.

To use as dessert, fill crêpes with chunky applesauce, peach preserves, strawberries, etc.

Use 1 1/2 cups buttermilk instead of regular milk and 1 tsp. baking soda instead of baking powder.

For twice as many crêpes, make 2 batches instead of doubling recipe.

"A bottle of wine begs to be shared; I have never met a miserly wine lover."
  Clifton Fadiman

"We may live without friends, we may live without books; but civilized man cannot live without cooks."
  Edward Bulwer Lytton

COURTSIDE

Alvarado Estates

Menu

CHINESE CHICKEN SALAD
GREEK SALAD
TACO SALAD
NASTURTIUM BUTTER FOR ROLLS
MACADAMIA CARAMEL PIE
KIR

Recipes

CHINESE CHICKEN SALAD

(Serves 8-10)

2 whole chicken breasts, cooked
3 Tbsp. toasted sesame seeds
1 6-oz. package slivered almonds, toasted
1/2 cup sunflower seeds
1/2 head Napa (Chinese) cabbage, thinly sliced
1/2 cup radishes, thinly sliced
3 green onions, chopped
1 package instant uncooked noodles
12 Chinese pea pods, cut in thirds
1 10-oz. package frozen petite peas, thawed
Garnish: Mandarin oranges

Shred chicken; add sesame seeds, almonds and sunflower seeds. Add cabbage, radishes and green onions. Crumble noodles and add, along with pea pods and thawed peas (do not cook). Toss with dressing and garnish with Mandarin oranges.

Dressing

1 tsp. sugar
1 tsp. salt
1/2 tsp. pepper
Flavoring packet from noodle package
1/3 cup oil
1/3 cup seasoned rice wine vinegar

GREEK SALAD

(Serves 8)

1 head green leaf lettuce, torn in bite-size pieces
2 large ripe tomatoes, sliced
1/2 cucumber, peeled and diced
1 cup pitted black olives
$1/2$-$3/4$ cup feta cheese, crumbled or in small pieces
2 cups cooked lamb, julienned (optional)

Dressing

1/2 cup olive oil
1/4 cup red wine vinegar
1/2 tsp. dried oregano, crumbled

Combine the first five (or six, if using lamb) ingredients in a large bowl. Combine dressing ingredients and toss with salad.

MACADAMIA CARAMEL PIE

(Serves 8)

Pastry

1/2 cup regular flour
1/4 cup cornstarch
1/4 tsp. salt
3/4 cup unsalted butter, at room temperature
1/3 cup granulated sugar
$1 1/4$ tsp. grated lemon zest

Continues on top of next page

Chocolate Coating

8 oz. semisweet chocolate, chopped
2 tsp. shortening

Filling

6 Tbsp. unsalted butter
1/3 cup packed dark brown sugar
1/4 cup honey
1 3/4 cups salted macadamia nuts
1 1/2 Tbsp. whipping cream

Caramel Glaze

8 oz. caramel candies (1 cup, packed)
1/4 cup water

Preheat oven to 350 degrees. Sift together flour, cornstarch and salt into a bowl and set aside. Combine butter, sugar and lemon zest in a large bowl. Beat until light and fluffy with an electric mixer on high speed. Reduce speed to low, add flour mixture and mix until the ingredients begin to gather into a dough. Turn onto floured board and roll out dough to fit 10-inch pie pan. Pierce all over with fork. Refrigerate 10 minutes. Place a piece of aluminum foil on top and up sides of dough. Partially fill with pie weights. Bake 10-15 minutes. Remove from oven. Take out foil and weights. Return to oven and bake 20 minutes more until it begins to color. Remove from oven. Leave oven set at 350 degrees.

To prepare the chocolate coating: Combine chocolate and shortening in the top pan of a double boiler. Melt over simmering water until smooth. Remove from heat and pour over crust.

Refrigerate until chocolate becomes almost hard.

To prepare the filling: Combine butter, brown sugar and honey in a heavy saucepan. Stir over medium-high heat and bring to a boil. Boil until thick, about 1 minute. Stir in nuts. Remove from heat and stir in cream. Spread the filling onto the crust. Bake until the caramel bubbles, about 20 minutes. Cool on a wire rack.

To prepare the caramel glaze: Combine caramels and water in small, heavy saucepan over low heat. Stir until the caramels melt and the mixture is smooth. Remove from heat.

Place 1 Tbsp. or more of caramel glaze on a plate, then place a piece of macadamia pie on top of the sauce. Serve.

KIR

(Serves 8)

3 1/2 cups (1 fifth) white Chablis
1 cup Crème de Cassis (black currant liqueur)

Combine well-chilled Chablis and Crème de Cassis. Pour into glasses and serve.

Recipes continue on page 87

HARBOR TERRACE

Point Loma

Menu

Citrus-Balsamic Salmon
Asparagus Spears with Chives
Fresh Mozzarella
Anchovies
Sun-Dried Tomatoes
Avocado Bread
Sour Cream Lemon Pie
White Pinot

CITRUS-BALSAMIC SALMON

CITRUS-BALSAMIC SALMON

(Serves 8)

Sauce

1 1/2 cups fresh orange juice
1 cup balsamic vinegar
4 Tbsp. extra virgin olive oil
2 anchovy fillets, minced, or 2-inch squirt
   of anchovy paste
4 Tbsp. minced onion
4 tsp. chopped parsley
4 tsp. chopped basil
4 tsp. chopped mint
4 Tbsp. minced orange zest
1/4 tsp. salt
Freshly ground black pepper

Salmon

8 6-oz. skinless salmon fillets
Salt and black pepper
4 Tbsp. olive oil

Preheat oven to 450 degrees. Combine sauce ingredients in pan and heat, uncovered, over low heat for 15 minutes. Season salmon with salt and pepper to taste. Heat olive oil in ovenproof skillet over high heat; add salmon, searing on both sides. Transfer to oven, cover with warm sauce, and bake for 10 minutes. Turn off oven, leaving fish in for 10 more minutes. Transfer fish to serving dish and keep warm.

If sauce needs thickening, place the pan over low heat and make a roux of 2 Tbsp. quick-mixing flour and 2 Tbsp. water; add to hot sauce and cook until thickened. Place extra sauce into serving dish and pass separately.

ASPARAGUS SPEARS WITH CHIVES

(Serves 8)

2 pounds asparagus
1 bunch chives

Rinse asparagus under cold water and break off tough ends. Steam until just tender; refresh under ice water. Divide the cooked asparagus into 8 bundles and tie with chives which have first been softened in hot water. Place on serving plate. Spoon a touch of the salmon sauce over the asparagus.

"All men are equal before fish."
   Herbert Hoover

AVOCADO BREAD

(Serves 6-8)

1 cup mashed avocado
2 eggs, beaten well
1/2 cup butter
1/4 cup sugar
2 tsp. lemon juice
2 tsp. baking powder
1 1/2 cups flour
1/2 tsp. salt
1 cup walnuts, chopped

Mix avocado with beaten eggs. Cream butter and sugar together and add all ingredients in order given. Pour batter into an 8 1/2 x 4 1/2 -inch greased and floured loaf pan. Bake at 350 degrees for 15 minutes. Lower temperature to 325 degrees and bake another 45 minutes. Cool on rack.

"Condiments are like old friends— highly thought of, but often taken for granted."
  Marilyn Kaytor

SOUR CREAM LEMON PIE

(Serves 8)

Baked 9-inch pie shell
1 cup sugar
3 1/2 Tbsp. cornstarch
1 Tbsp. grated lemon rind
1/2 cup lemon juice
3 egg yolks, lightly beaten
1 cup whole milk (not skim)
1/4 cup butter
1 cup sour cream
1/2 cup whipping cream, whipped
   (optional: add 1 tsp. sugar)
Lemon, sliced thinly
Shredded coconut, toasted

Mix sugar, cornstarch, rind, lemon juice, yolks and milk in 1-quart microwave-proof measuring cup with hand beater on slow. Microwave on full power, with saucer over cup, for 2 minutes. Stir and repeat twice more — that is, 2+2+2 minutes, stirring each time — 6 minutes or less, until thickened. Remove and add butter. Let cool in cup. Add sour cream, blending in with rubber scraper. Pour into baked pie shell. Refrigerate about 30 minutes, then cover with whipped cream. Garnish with very thin, twisted lemon slices, or shredded coconut toasted in shallow pan at 350 degrees for 5 minutes. Chill pie.

CONTEMPORARY CURRY

Menu

9-BOY CURRY
FRIED RICE
FRUIT CHUTNEY
MINT SLAW
BISCUIT BITS
LICHEES IN CHAMPAGNE

Point Loma

COUNTRY COMFORT

Menu

MEATLOAF
MASHED POTATOES
CALIFORNIA CARROTS
GARLIC ZUCCHINI
POPOVERS
FRESH LEMON ICE IN LEMON SHELLS
GAMAY

Rancho Santa Fe

Recipes

9-BOY CURRY

(Serves 8)

4 cups cooked meat (chicken, lamb or beef), cut
   in 1-inch cubes

2 tart green apples, peeled and chopped

1 onion, chopped

4 cloves garlic, pressed

3 Tbsp. butter

2 tsp. salt

2 Tbsp. curry powder

4 tsp. fresh ginger, chopped

1/2 cup flour

28 oz. canned coconut milk

2 cups half-and-half or whole milk

   Cook apples, onion and garlic in butter until golden and tender. Mix in salt, curry powder, ginger and flour. Add coconut milk and half-and-half (or milk). Stir until bubbling and slightly thickened. Add cubed meat. Heat through and serve over rice.

9-Boy Condiments

Chutney

Sliced bananas

Raisins

Chopped peanuts

Cooked, grated egg

Flaked coconut

Mandarin oranges

Chopped green onions

Crisp bacon, crumbled

FRIED RICE

(Serves 8)

8 cups cooked rice

4 large eggs

1 tsp. dry sherry

2/3 cup thinly sliced green onions, including tops

2 tsp. salt

1/2 cup corn oil

   Place rice in large bowl and break up any lumps. Break eggs directly onto rice. Add sherry , onions and salt. Mix thoroughly. Pour oil into wok and place over medium-high heat. Heat until hot, but not smoking. Turn rice mixture into pan. Increase temperature to high. Stir constantly, 3-10 minutes. Serve hot.

"An expert is like the bottom of a double boiler. It shoots off a lot of steam, but it never really knows what's cooking."
   Unknown

Recipes continue on page 87

Recipes

MEATLOAF

(Serves 8)

2 pounds lean ground round beef
1/2 cup crushed saltine crackers and 3/4 cup soft bread crumbs
1 cup chopped mushrooms
1/2 cup shredded carrots
1 cup chopped onion
2 eggs
1 1/2 cups chili sauce
2 tsp. salt
1/2 tsp. pepper
2 tsp. Worcestershire sauce
10 saltine cracker squares
5 strips thin bacon, fat cut from edge and end

Grease a 9x5-inch loaf pan. Combine all ingredients, except last 10 saltines and bacon, and pack into pan. Crush the 10 saltine squares and sprinkle over the top. Lay bacon on top. Bake for 45 minutes to 1 hour at 350 degrees.

MASHED POTATOES

(Serves 8-12)

12 baking potatoes, boiled and mashed
2 tsp. onion salt
1/2 tsp. white pepper
1 cup sour cream, room temperature or warmed in microwave

8 oz. cream cheese, room temperature or warmed in microwave
1/4 cup butter, melted

Combine all ingredients and place in casserole. Bake at 350 degrees for 45 minutes to 1 hour. Can be made a day ahead and refrigerated.

CALIFORNIA CARROTS

(Serves 8)

1/3 cup frozen orange juice, undiluted
1/3 cup Marsala wine
1 Tbsp. light brown sugar
1 Tbsp. butter
5 cups carrots, processed on fine shoestring disk, or grated

Blend together juice, wine, sugar and butter in pan. Add carrots and heat through on range top or in microwave. Salt and pepper to taste.

GARLIC ZUCCHINI

(Serves 8)

3 Tbsp. butter
3 cloves garlic, pressed
6 zucchini, processed on shoestring disk
1 tsp. powdered nutmeg
1 tsp. salt
1/2 tsp. pepper

Sauté garlic in butter until golden. Heat zucchini in the garlic butter in microwave for 2 minutes, or until hot. Sprinkle with seasoning and serve.

Recipes continue on page 88

UN ALMUERZO MEXICANO

Del Cerro

Menu

ROASTED CORN GUACAMOLE
CHICKEN ENCHILADAS
TOMATILLO SAUCE
SALSA
CACTUS SALAD
BUÑELAS
MARGARITAS

Recipes

ROASTED CORN GUACAMOLE

(Serves 8)

1 cup fresh corn or frozen corn (thawed)
2 Tbsp. corn oil
3 large avocados, finely chopped
1 large tomato, finely chopped
1/2 cup cilantro, finely chopped
2 Tbsp. red onion, finely chopped
1 tsp. pickled jalapeño pepper, finely chopped
1 tsp. garlic, pressed
1/2 cup canned black beans
2 Tbsp. fresh lime juice
1 tsp. cider vinegar
1 $1/2$ tsp. salt
1/4 tsp. cumin
1   10-oz. package blue corn chips

Preheat oven to 450 degrees. Toss the corn with 1 Tbsp. oil. Roast on cookie sheet 7 minutes, tossing several times. Cool. Place in bowl with last 1 Tbsp. oil and remaining ingredients, except chips. Mix and refrigerate several hours. Serve with chips.

CHICKEN ENCHILADAS

(Serves 6)

Tomatillo Sauce

1 medium onion, chopped
1 Tbsp. corn or safflower oil
1 pound fresh tomatillos, husked, or 16 oz. canned tomatillos, drained

1 Tbsp. canned green chili, peeled and chopped
2 Tbsp. fresh coriander, minced
Salt and freshly ground black pepper to taste

In a frying pan, cook onion in oil until translucent; set aside. If using fresh tomatillos, cook in boiling, salted water to cover until tender, about 10 minutes. Drain. Purée tomatillos in blender with just enough water to make a smooth sauce. Add to onions. Add chili and fresh coriander and cook, stirring occasionally, until slightly thickened. Season to taste with salt and pepper. Makes about 2 cups of sauce.

Enchiladas

Corn or safflower oil for frying
12 corn tortillas
1 $1/2$ pounds cooked chicken
2 bunches green onions, chopped
2 Tbsp. butter
12 oz. Monterey Jack cheese, shredded
   (about 3 cups)
1 can (5 3/4-oz.) pitted jumbo black olives
1 large avocado, peeled and sliced
1 large tomato, cut in wedges
Sour cream

Heat 1/8-inch oil in a large frying pan and fry tortillas until lightly browned on the edges; drain on absorbent paper. Sauté onions in butter until soft. Spread about 1/2-cup of chicken in a ribbon on each tortilla, sprinkle with onion and about 1 Tbsp. of tomatillo sauce and roll up. Arrange seam-side down on greased

Continues on top of next page

baking dish. Lightly spoon tomatillo sauce over enchiladas and sprinkle with cheese. Bake in preheated 400-degree oven for 15 minutes, or until heated through. Garnish with olives, avocado slices and tomato wedges on top. Pass around sour cream.

SALSA

(Makes 5 cups)

2 Tbsp. red wine vinegar
1/2 tsp. freshly ground black pepper
1/8 tsp. ground cumin
1 Tbsp. corn oil
2 jalapeño peppers, seeded, deveined and finely chopped (1/4 cup)
1/2 cup jícama
3 medium tomatoes, peeled, seeded and diced (2 cups)
1/2 cup onion, finely chopped
1 1/2 cups corn kernels
1/4 cup chopped fresh cilantro
2 whole green onions, chopped
2 tsp. fresh lime juice

Combine first 5 ingredients. Add remaining ingredients and chill for several hours. Serve.

CACTUS SALAD

(Serves 6)

1 cup nopalitos (cactus leaves, available in glass jars in Mexican food section of supermarkets), chopped
1/4 cup cilantro, chopped
1 avocado, peeled and cubed

1 cup garbanzo beans, drained
3 plum tomatoes, chopped
2 garlic cloves, chopped
4 green onions, chopped
1 small can sliced ripe olives, drained
1/2 cucumber, chopped
Salt and pepper to taste

Dressing

3 Tbsp. lime juice
2 Tbsp. olive oil

Mix all salad ingredients together and chill until serving. Combine dressing ingredients, mix well and pour over salad.

BUÑELAS

(Serves 8)

8 small wheat tortillas
Oil for frying
Sugar
Cinnamon
1 can apple pie filling
1 quart vanilla ice cream

Deep-fry tortillas and mold, while warm, over back of muffin pans to make cups. Remove and sprinkle with sugar and cinnamon, while still warm, until lightly coated. Fill with apple pie filling and top with a scoop of ice cream.

Recipes continue on page 89

AFTER GOLF

Morgan Run

Menu

Menu

Cornish Game Hens in Grand Marnier Sauce
Wild Rice
Spinach-Jícama Salad
Double Corn Muffins
Caramel Apple Crisp
Lemonade

CORNISH GAME HENS IN GRAND MARNIER SAUCE

(Serves 8)

4 Cornish Game Hens
2/3 cup orange juice
1/4 cup lemon juice
Grated rind of 1 orange
1 Tbsp. curry
1 tsp. salt
3 garlic cloves, pressed
1/4 cup Grand Marnier
3 Tbsp. Dijon mustard
1/2 cup honey
Garnish: Mandarin oranges

Split game hens in half. Mix all remaining ingredients and pour over hens. Cover legs with foil. Bake at 350 degrees for 1 hour. If hens become too brown, cover for rest of baking time. Garnish with Mandarin oranges.

WILD RICE

(Serves 8)

1 cup wild rice
3 cups boiling chicken broth
1 cup onion, chopped
1 Tbsp. butter or margarine
1 cup water chestnuts, sliced
1 Tbsp. grated orange rind
Salt and pepper to taste

Place rice in strainer and wash thoroughly in cold running water. Bring broth to a boil and add the cleaned rice. Reduce heat and simmer, covered, for 40-50 minutes (until most of the rice has popped). While rice is cooking, melt butter in a pan. Add onion and sauté until translucent; set aside until rice is cooked.

Drain rice and add onion, orange rind and water chestnuts. Season with salt and pepper.

"I'd rather have roses on my table than diamonds around my neck."
Emma Goldman

SPINACH-JÍCAMA SALAD

(Serves 8)

2 bunches fresh baby spinach
6 green onions, sliced in 1/4-inch pieces
1 cup jícama, peeled and diced
8 bacon slices, cooked and crumbled
1 cup pistachio nuts, chopped

Dressing

2 fresh garlic cloves, pressed
1/4 tsp. dry mustard
1 tsp. salt
1/3 cup catsup
1/3 cup sugar
1/3 cup vinegar (mixture of balsamic and
   red wine vinegars)
1 cup olive oil
Dash ground cloves
Dash lemon pepper (generous)

Combine all dressing ingredients and blend well with wire whip.

Wash and dry spinach, remove stems and tear into bite-size pieces. Add green onion, jícama and bacon. To serve, add desired amount of dressing and toss gently.

Garnish with pistachios.

DOUBLE CORN MUFFINS

(Make 8 muffins)

Add 1 cup thawed whole-kernel corn to a favorite cornbread recipe that makes 8 muffins.

CARAMEL APPLE CRISP

(Serves 10-12)

10 green apples
2 cups all-purpose flour, unsifted
3/4 cup brown sugar
3/4 cup granulated sugar
Dash cinnamon
1 cup butter (cold)

Peel apples, cut in half and remove the cores. Cut into 1/4-inch slices. Lightly press apples into shallow baking dish, making a fairly even surface.

In electric mixer, using paddle attachment, combine flour, brown sugar, sugar and cinnamon. Cut butter into 16 squares and add while mixing, until mixture resembles coarse meal.

Sprinkle mixture evenly over apples and bake at 325 degrees for 45 minutes.

Dust with powdered sugar. Serve with caramel sauce.

Caramel Sauce

Scant 1 cup sugar
1/2 cup water
1/4 cup butter (cold)
1 cup heavy cream

Combine sugar and water in a heavy saucepan and bring to a boil. Remove from heat when it reaches a brown color or 320 degrees on a candy thermometer.

Add butter and stir with a whip until dissolved. Add cream and return mixture to heat for 1 minute, stirring to combine.

Remove from heat, strain and keep warm.

SURF AND SAND PICNIC

Fletcher Cove

Menu

CRAB PIZZA

FRESH FRUIT

COOKIES
PRALINES
OATMEAL DROPS
APRICOT NUT BARS

BEER

Recipes

CRAB PIZZA

(Serves 8)

1/4 cup mayonnaise
1/4 cup sour cream
1 tsp. lemon juice
1/2 tsp. Tabasco
1/2 pound crabmeat
1/4 cup Parmesan cheese, grated
1 cup grated Swiss cheese
Olive oil
1 12-inch Italian pizza crust (thin-style)
6 oz. small cooked shrimp
1/3 cup scallions, chopped
Paprika

Preheat oven to 450 degrees.
Combine first four ingredients in medium bowl. Add crabmeat and Parmesan and Swiss cheeses.
Oil pizza pan and place crust on pan. Paint crust with olive oil. Spread crab mixture over crust. Make a design with the shrimp on top. Sprinkle with scallions and paprika. Bake until topping is puffed and brown, 10-15 minutes. Cut into small wedges and serve immediately.

PRALINES

(Makes about 35)

1 cup butter (not margarine)
1 cup brown sugar
1 cup chopped pecans
Graham crackers

Bring butter and sugar to boil for 2 minutes, stirring constantly. Remove from heat and add nuts. Line ungreased 10x15-inch jelly roll pan with crackers. Pour mixture over and bake at 350 degrees for 10 minutes. Cool for 10 minutes. Cut into squares or triangles.

"Man's hunger is in relation to food; zest is in relation to life."
Bertrand Russell

OATMEAL DROPS

(Makes about 6 dozen)

1 cup raisins
1/2 cup hot water
2 cups flour, sifted
1 tsp. soda
1 tsp. salt
1 tsp. nutmeg
1 tsp. cinnamon
2 cups rolled oats
1 cup brown sugar
1/2 cup chopped nuts (optional)
2 eggs
3/4 cup vegetable oil
1 tsp. vanilla

Soak raisins in hot water; set aside.
Sift flour with soda, salt and spices into mixing bowl. Blend in rolled oats, sugar and nuts. Break eggs into raisin mixture and mix. Add oil and vanilla. Pour into dry mixture and stir until just blended.

Drop by spoonfuls onto ungreased baking sheet. Bake at 350 degrees for 10-13 minutes.

APRICOT NUT BARS

(Makes about 16)

2/3 cup dried apricots
1/2 cup butter
1/4 cup granulated sugar
1 cup flour, sifted

Rinse apricots and cover with water. Boil 10 minutes. Drain, cool and chop. Set aside. Grease 8x8x2-inch pan. Mix butter, sugar, and flour until crumbly. Place into pan and bake at 350 degrees until lightly browned.

Topping

1/3 cup flour, sifted
1/2 tsp. baking powder
1/4 tsp. salt
1 cup brown sugar
2 eggs, beaten
1/2 tsp. vanilla
1/2 cup chopped nuts
Powdered sugar

Sift together flour, baking powder and salt. Beat brown sugar into eggs. Add sifted flour mixture and mix well. Add vanilla, apricots and nuts. Spread over baked layer and bake at 350 degrees for 30 minutes. Cool in pan and cut into bars. Sprinkle with powdered sugar.

ALL CHOCOLATE TEA

Del Rayo Estates

Menu

Chocolate Fondue
Chocolate-Orange Pecan Pie
Chocolate Crème Brulée
Baked Alaska
Guilt-Free Chocolate Sauce
Microwave Fudge
Brownies
Mint Surprise Cookies
Petite Sirah or Tokay or Madeira

Recipes

CHOCOLATE FONDUE

(Serves 8)

12 oz. semisweet chocolate bits
1/4 cup milk or half-and-half
1/4 cup orange or raspberry liqueur or Crème de Cacao
2 Tbsp. butter

Combine chocolate and milk in top of double boiler over barely simmering water. Stir often until smoothly melted. Add butter and stir until melted. Add liqueur and transfer to chafing dish.

Dippers for Fondue:

Strawberries, whole with stems
Kiwi, quartered
Banana chunks
Bite-size apples, pears, pineapple, melon, grapes, cherries, marshmallows, pound cake or dried fruit

CHOCOLATE-ORANGE PECAN PIE

(Serves 8-10)

Ready-made 9-inch pie crust
6 oz. semisweet chocolate bits
2 cups pecan halves

Preheat oven to 350 degrees. Place layer of chocolate bits and pecan halves on pie crust.

Filling

4 eggs
1 cup dark brown sugar
1/2 cup butter, melted
2 Tbsp. flour
1 Tbsp. vanilla
2 Tbsp. bourbon or dark rum
1 tsp. grated orange peel

Whisk eggs together with the rest of ingredients. Pour mixture over chocolate and nuts in pie shell. Bake at 350 degrees for 1/2 hour, or until set when filling puffs and no longer moves in the center when pie is shaken.

CHOCOLATE DECORATIONS FOR CAKE

Ruffle: Turn a cookie sheet upside down. Spread a 3-inch strip of melted semisweet chocolate (12 oz.) along its length. Cool and refrigerate until just set, not hard, about 3 minutes. Using wide spatula with tip under chocolate, push down length of sheet to form ruffle. Ruffles break if too cold and stick if too warm. Press ruffles onto frosted cake as desired.

Leaf: Using inner leaves of a small red cabbage, paint their backs with a brush dipped in melted semisweet chocolate. Avoid covering the edges. Place in refrigerator. When hard, peel off chocolate leaves and place upright on top of frosted cake.

CHOCOLATE CRÈME BRULÉE

(Serves 8)

10 large egg yolks
1 1/4 cups sugar
4 cups whipping cream
2 Tbsp. vanilla
4 oz. semisweet chocolate, chopped

Preheat oven to 300 degrees. Beat yolks and 1 cup sugar in large bowl. Bring cream to simmer in heavy small saucepan. Whisk hot cream into yolks. Whisk in vanilla. Divide chocolate among eight 3/4-cup custard cups. Ladle custard over chocolate. Place cups in baking pan. Add enough hot water to pan to come halfway up sides of cups. Bake until custards are just set in center, about 55 minutes. Remove custards from water and cool. Cover and refrigerate overnight.

Preheat broiler. Sprinkle 1/2 Tbsp. sugar over each custard. Broil until sugar caramelizes, about 2 minutes. Cool 5 minutes and serve.

BAKED ALASKA

(Serves 8+)

30 round chocolate sandwich-style cookies, with vanilla filling removed
1/4 cup butter, melted
1/2 gallon Mandarin orange ice cream, or coffee, butter brickle, etc.
1-1 1/2 cups chocolate sauce

4 egg whites
1/4 tsp. cream of tartar
6 Tbsp. sugar
1/2 tsp. vanilla

Place cookies in processor or blender; pour in melted butter and blend. Pat into 10-inch pie pan. Bake at 350 degrees for 8 minutes. Cool crust. Fill pan with ice cream, then freeze. Heat oven to 450 degrees. Whip egg whites until frothy. Add cream of tartar and beat until whites peak. Slowly beat in the sugar. Add vanilla. Wet a plank of wood to place under the pie. Turn on broiler. Take frozen pie out of freezer and cover with meringue. Place on wet wood plank and put under hot broiler with meringue 4-6 inches from heating element. Close oven and watch until the meringue turns golden. Remove quickly to freezer. Can be made a few hours before serving.

GUILT-FREE CHOCOLATE SAUCE

(Makes about 1 1/2 cups)

1 cup cocoa
3/4 cup sugar
1/2 tsp. salt
1 Tbsp. cornstarch
1/2 cup corn syrup
1/2 cup canned skim milk
2 tsp. brandy

Mix dry ingredients. Add corn syrup and canned milk. Cook 15 minutes over hot water, stirring until thickened. Cool and add brandy. Refrigerate until ready to use. May be heated for an ice cream sauce or as a low-calorie fondue.

Recipes continue on page 89

SHERRY TEA

La Jolla

Menu

CRANBERRY BAKED BRIE
APRICOT-ALMOND BRIE
SPICED PECANS
FRITTATA VERTÉ
CHEESE PUFFS
CAVIAR MOUSSE
ARTICHOKE ROUNDS
HEARTS OF PALM
TRIFLE

Recipes

CRANBERRY BAKED BRIE

(Serves 8-10)

1 1/2 cups dried cranberries
1/2 cup hot water
1/2 cup brown sugar
1/3 cup currants
1/4 tsp. each dry mustard, allspice, cardamom, cloves and ginger
1 pound round Brie

Preheat oven to 325 degrees.

Combine dried cranberries with hot water in a saucepan. Add brown sugar and mix until sugar dissolves. Set aside to soak, about 10 minutes. Cut out the top crust of the Brie, leaving a 1/4-inch border. Combine the currants and seasonings and add to the cranberry mixture. Cook on low heat until liquid is absorbed. Place the Brie in an ovenproof serving dish with sides. Put the cranberry mixture on top of the Brie in the circle. Bake at 325 degrees for 10-15 minutes, or until the Brie melts and bubbles. Serve warm with crackers or toasted bread rounds.

APRICOT-ALMOND BRIE

(Serves 8-10)

1 pound round Brie
1/2 cup sliced almonds
1-2 Tbsp. butter
1/4 cup brown sugar
1/2 cup thick (lots of fruit) apricot preserves

Cut out the top crust of the Brie, leaving a 1/4-inch border. Place Brie in ovenproof serving dish with sides. Sauté almonds in butter until golden. Cover the Brie with brown sugar, then cover with preserves. Sprinkle with almonds. Bake at 325 degrees for 10-15 minutes, or until Brie melts and bubbles.

SPICED PECANS

(Makes 2 cups)

3 Tbsp. unsalted butter
1/2 tsp. salt
1 1/2 tsp. cinnamon
1/4 tsp. cayenne pepper
Dash of Tabasco sauce
2 cups pecans

Preheat oven to 300 degrees. Melt butter in heavy saucepan over low heat. Mix in salt, cinnamon, cayenne and Tabasco. Place pecans in medium bowl. Pour butter mixture over and toss. Spread nuts on heavy cookie sheet. Bake until crisp, about 15 minutes. Cool and serve.

FRITTATA VERTÉ

(Makes 28-30 pieces)

1/2 10-oz. package frozen chopped spinach (thawed and squeezed dry)
1 cup ricotta cheese

Continues on top of next page

3/4 cup Parmesan cheese, grated
2/3 cup chopped mushrooms
2 Tbsp. chopped onion
1/2 tsp. oregano
1/4 tsp. salt
1 egg
Optional: sliced pepperoni sausage and sour cream

Mix spinach with ricotta cheese, Parmesan cheese, mushrooms, onion, oregano, salt and egg. Lightly grease 7x11-inch pan. Spoon in cheese and spinach mixture. Bake at 375 degrees for 20 minutes, or until a light golden color. Cool 10 minutes and cut into squares. Garnish with pieces of pepperoni and dabs of sour cream, if desired. Squares may be frozen. To reheat, bake at 375 degrees for 6 minutes, or until piping hot. May be served warm or cold.

CHEESE PUFFS

(Makes 48)

1 cup black olives, chopped
1/2 cup chopped green onions (with tops)
1 1/2 cups sharp Cheddar cheese, shredded
1/2 cup light mayonnaise
1/2 tsp. curry powder
6 English muffins

Mix together first 5 ingredients. Split muffins and brush off crumbs. Spread cheese mixture on muffins and broil until cheese melts. Cut into quarters. Serve hot.

CAVIAR MOUSSE

(Serves 6-8)

3/4 cup light sour cream
1/4 cup chopped onions (optional)
3 hard-boiled eggs, halved
3 Tbsp. light mayonnaise
4 tsp. lemon juice
1/2 tsp. salt
1/2 tsp. Worcestershire sauce
1/4 tsp. white pepper
2-3 drops Tabasco sauce, or to taste
1 1/2 tsp. unflavored gelatin
2-3 oz. caviar or black lumpfish

Mix everything in food processor, except gelatin and caviar. Sprinkle gelatin over 2 Tbsp. cold water to soften; then dissolve in microwave. Stir into sour cream mixture. Gently add caviar; put into mold and chill. Serve with crackers.

"Wine is constant proof that God loves us and loves to see us happy."
  Ben Franklin

Recipes continue on page 90

CHILD'S TEA PARTY

Point Loma

Menu

FLOWER COOKIES
ICE CREAM CONE CAKES
PAINTED COOKIES
FINGER COOKIES

CANDIED FLOWERS
SWEETHEART SANDWICHES
SHERBET PUNCH
FRUIT PUNCH

Recipes

FLOWER COOKIES

(Makes about 3 dozen)

1/2 cup butter, softened
1 cup sugar
1 1/3 cups flour
3/4 tsp. baking powder
1/4 tsp. salt
1 tsp. vanilla

Preheat oven to 350 degrees. Combine all ingredients and beat until blended. Drop by rounded teaspoonfuls onto an ungreased cookie sheet 1 1/2 inches apart. Bake 10-12 minutes.

Syrup

3 strips orange peel
1 cup sugar
1/3 cup water

In saucepan, boil peel, sugar and water on high heat (do not stir) until syrup reaches 238 degrees (syrup must cover thermometer base). Discard peel; let syrup stand undisturbed until just warm, about 40 minutes.

Garnish

On top of each cookie, place 1 tsp. syrup, then press 1 or 2 flowers (use tiny violets, nasturtiums, pansies or roses) into syrup and let stand for 4 hours.

ICE CREAM CONE CAKES

(Makes 3 dozen)

1 box cake mix
3 dozen 3-inch flat-bottomed ice cream cones
1-pound can light frosting, or about 1 1/2 cups homemade frosting
Candy sprinkles or other cake decorations

Preheat oven to 350 degrees. Prepare cake batter according to package instructions. Fill each cone half-full with batter (about 2 Tbsp.) and place on baking sheet with space between cones. Bake 25 minutes, or until toothpick inserted comes out clean. Cool. Frost; decorate as desired.

SWEETHEART SANDWICHES

Cut crust from bread. Using cookie cutter, cut bread into heart shapes. Spread cream cheese on one heart and top with another. Thinly slice strawberries and place one or two slices on top of each heart sandwich.

"I doubt whether the world holds for anyone a more soul-stirring surprise than the first adventure with ice cream."
Heywood Broun

PAINTED COOKIES

(Makes 3 dozen)

Use Flower Cookie recipe

<u>Glaze</u>

6 Tbsp. water
1 pound powdered sugar

Mix water and sugar. Spread on warm flower cookies. Dry 8-24 hours. Paint with watercolor brush dipped in undiluted food coloring.

FINGER COOKIES

(Makes 12 dozen)

1 cup flour
1/3 cup powdered sugar
1/2 cup butter, softened
2 tsp. vanilla
1/2 cup pecans, finely chopped

Mix all ingredients together. Knead with fingers until almost stiff. With greased hands, pinch off a piece of dough and roll it on the palm of the left hand in a snake shape. Curve into crescents on a buttered cookie sheet. Bake at 325 degrees about 10 minutes. Dust well with powdered sugar.

CANDIED FLOWERS

Rose petals, violets, orange blossoms, lilacs, jasmine
1 egg white
Superfine sugar

Beat egg white with a few drops of water until a fine froth is formed.

Sprinkle sugar in a thick layer over a cookie sheet. Dip pastry brush into froth and paint blossoms. Sprinkle with sugar to lightly coat. Place blossoms facedown into sugar so petals dry spread out. Sprinkle more sugar over thin spots. Dry several hours.

SHERBET PUNCH

12 oz. frozen orange juice, undiluted, thawed
2 quarts ginger ale
1 quart orange or lime sherbet
Strawberries and orange slices

Combine orange juice and ginger ale in punch bowl. Float scoops of orange or lime sherbet in punch. Add strawberries and slices of orange to garnish. Makes 36 1/2-cup servings.

FRUIT PUNCH

1 pint Hawaiian punch concentrate
6 oz. frozen lemonade
6 oz. frozen orange juice
1 quart soda
Strawberries and orange slices

Dilute first three ingredients according to directions; combine in large punch bowl over ice mold. Add soda just before serving. Garnish with strawberries and slices of orange.

"Enjoy your ice cream while it's on your plate—that's my philosophy."
Thorton Wilder

HOLIDAY TEA

Point Loma

Menu

SANDWICH COMBINATIONS
CREAM SCONES WITH ORANGE MARMALADE
CALIFORNIA CHEESECAKE
BISCUITS DE NOEL
WORLD'S FINEST ROCA CANDY
MICROWAVE PEANUT BRITTLE
PECAN DIVINES
LEMON COOKIE BARS
MINT TEA

Recipes

SANDWICH COMBINATIONS

Curried chicken with peanuts on white bread.

Tomato with basil and mayonnaise on whole-grain bread.

Avocado with sprouts and walnuts on whole-wheat bread.

Stilton cheese crumbled over pear slices on oatmeal bread.

Sugar-cured ham with thinly sliced pineapple on Hawaiian bread.

Cucumber slices with lemon mayonnaise on dill bread.

CREAM SCONES WITH ORANGE MARMALADE

(Makes 1 dozen)

1 Tbsp. baking powder
1/2 tsp. salt
3 Tbsp. sugar
2 cups flour
1/2 cup butter
2 large eggs
1/2 cup cream or half-and-half
1/2 cup currants
3 Tbsp. vanilla

Sift dry ingredients. Cut in butter. Add remaining ingredients. Turn onto floured board and knead gently. Cut into circles about 1-inch thick. Brush with mixture of egg yolk and cream. Place on cookie sheet lined with buttered foil. Bake at 450 degrees 10-15 minutes. Serve warm with honey butter made with sweet butter, honey and vanilla, or orange marmalade.

ORANGE MARMALADE

(Makes 6 cups)

4 medium oranges with good, smooth skins
1 medium lemon with good, smooth skin
1 1/2 cups water
1/4 tsp. baking soda
6 cups sugar (approximately)
1 box fruit pectin

Peel fruit and remove most of white pulp. Finely chop peel of oranges and lemon. Add water and baking soda. Bring to a boil, cover and simmer 10 minutes. Remove the membranes from orange sections, saving juice and fruit. Combine fruit, juice and orange and lemon peels in water. Cover and simmer for 20 minutes. Measure cups of cooked mixture. Add 2 cups of sugar per cup of fruit mix. Heat and cook for 5 minutes. Remove from heat and add fruit pectin according to directions on box. Skim off any froth and mix well. Seal in hot, sterilized glass containers.

CALIFORNIA CHEESECAKE

(Serves 8)

32 graham crackers squares
1/4 cup butter, softened
9 oz. cream cheese, room temperature
2 eggs
1/2 cup sugar
1 tsp. vanilla
1 Tbsp. grated orange rind
1 cup sour cream
2 Tbsp. sugar
1 tsp. vanilla

Preheat oven to 350 degrees. Crush graham crackers and mix with butter. Pat into 9-inch pie tin. Bake for 5 minutes and cool.

Mash cream cheese and mix with eggs, sugar and vanilla. Beat until smoothly blended. Add orange rind. Pour into cool pie shell. Bake 15 minutes at 300 degrees. Cool 5 minutes. Blend sour cream, sugar and vanilla. Pour over cake. Bake 5 minutes at 300 degrees. Cool in refrigerator overnight.

BISCUITS DE NOEL

(Makes 24 slices)

1 cup sweet butter
3/4 cup brown sugar
1/2 tsp. vanilla
1/8 tsp. salt
2 1/2 cups all-purpose flour
1 cup slivered almonds
1/2 cup red cherries, cut in quarters
1/2 cup green cherries, cut in quarters

Cream butter and add brown sugar, vanilla, salt, flour, almonds and cherries. Shape into a roll and put into refrigerator overnight. Cut into thin slices and bake on a greased cookie sheet at 375 degrees for 10 minutes.

WORLD'S FINEST ROCA CANDY

1 pound milk chocolate, grated or finely chopped in food processor
2 1/4 cups blanched almonds, finely chopped by hand (not powdery)

Sprinkle half the nuts, then half the chocolate, evenly onto jelly roll pan.

2 cups butter
2 cups granulated sugar

Cook over medium heat, stirring slowly and constantly, to exactly 300 degrees on candy thermometer (about 15 minutes). At 300 degrees, immediately remove from heat and pour over chocolate and nuts. Add last half of chocolate, then nuts, sprinkling evenly over sugar-butter mixture while still hot enough to melt the chocolate. Chill in refrigerator; break into bite-size pieces.

"The biggest seller is cookbooks and the second is diet books — how not to eat what you've just learned how to cook."
Andy Rooney

Recipes continue on page 91

Continued from page 7

MIXED GREENS WITH DRIED CRANBERRIES AND PECANS

(Serves 8)

Mixed greens

1 cup dried cranberries
1 cup chopped pecans

Dressing

1/4 cup olive oil
1/4 cup raspberry vinegar
2 tsp. Dijon mustard
1 tsp. water

Fill salad bowl with mixed greens. Add dried cranberries and pecans. Combine olive oil, raspberry vinegar, Dijon mustard and water. Toss greens with dressing.

PARMESAN STICKS

1 cup freshly grated Parmesan
1 cup crushed corn flakes
1 loaf very thin white bread
1 1/4 cups butter, melted (may need more)

Freeze bread. Mix cheese and corn flakes. Remove 2 slices of bread at a time from freezer. Trim crusts, dip in butter, then cheese mixture. Place on cookie sheet and cut into strips. Bake at 350 degrees for 7-8 minutes until golden brown.

These keep for several weeks in refrigerator or can be frozen and reheated.

Good with soup or salad.

LEMON CREAM CAKE

(Serves 8-10)

6 egg yolks, beaten
3/4 cup sugar
1/2 cup lemon juice
1/4 cup orange juice
1 1/2 tsp. grated lemon peel
1 envelope plus 1/2 tsp. gelatin
1/4 cup water
6 egg whites
3/4 cup sugar
1 large angel food cake

Topping

2 cups whipping cream
2 tsp. sugar
1 tsp. vanilla

Make custard of egg yolks, 3/4 cup sugar, lemon and orange juices and lemon peel. Cook over hot, not boiling, water (in double boiler) until mixture coats the spoon. Remove from heat and add gelatin that has been softened in 1/4 cup water. Let mixture cool.

Beat egg whites until stiff, adding the remaining 3/4 cup sugar. Fold into cooled custard mixture.

Break angel food cake into bite-size pieces and thoroughly fold into custard mixture. Pour into a greased tube cake pan and let set in the refrigerator for 4 hours or overnight.

When ready to serve, turn onto a cake plate and cover with topping.

Continued from page 19

COFFEE TORTONI

(Serves 8)

1 egg white
1 Tbsp. instant coffee
2 Tbsp. sugar
1 cup whipping cream
1/3 cup sugar
1 tsp. vanilla
1/8 tsp. almond extract
1/4 cup buttered almonds

Beat egg white until it forms soft peaks. Add instant coffee and sugar. Beat cream in a separate bowl. Add 1/3 cup sugar, vanilla and almond extract. Fold almonds into this mixture. Fold egg white mixture into cream mixture. Put into cupcake papers placed in muffin tins. Freeze for 24 hours.

Continued from page 31

CAESAR SALAD

(Serves 4)

2 slices pumpernickel bread
1 Tbsp. olive oil
1 large clove garlic, pressed
1 head romaine, torn into pieces

Special Dressing

1 clove garlic, pressed
1 tsp. Dijon mustard
1/2 tsp. Worcestershire sauce
1/4 tsp. salt
1/2 tsp. pepper
2 Tbsp. mayonnaise
2 Tbsp. lemon juice
2-inch squirt of anchovy paste

1/4 cup olive oil
3 Tbsp. Parmesan cheese, grated

Mix olive oil with pressed garlic clove and brush on bread. Toast in 400-degree oven until crisp. Cut into 1/2-inch cubes and set croutons aside.

In a small bowl, beat together garlic, Dijon, Worcestershire, salt, pepper, mayonnaise, lemon juice and anchovy paste. Whisk in the oil, and continue to beat until dressing gets thick. Stir in Parmesan cheese and pour dressing over romaine. Add croutons, toss and serve on chilled plates.

HERB BREAD

(Serves 8)

4 Tbsp. butter
1/4 tsp. garlic powder
1/2 tsp. basil
1/2 tsp. oregano
1 package bread sticks
Parmesan cheese

Melt butter and combine with seasonings. Pour half into bottom of an 8-inch square pan. Break bread sticks to fit pan in one layer. Brush remaining butter on top. Bake uncovered at 200 degrees for 45 minutes. Turn sticks and sprinkle with Parmesan. Bake 45 minutes more.

Instead of bread sticks, one of the following could be substituted:

1. 8 flour tortillas cut in quarters and brushed with herb mixture and baked at 300 degrees for 30 minutes.

2. 10-inch round brown-and-serve loaf, slashed, brushed with herb mix and baked at 350 degrees for 30 minutes.

Recipes continue on page 86

Continued from page 85

CARROT CAKE

(Serves 12)

1 1/2 cups oil
2 cups sugar
4 eggs, beaten
2 cups sifted flour
2 tsp. cinnamon
2 tsp. baking powder
2 tsp. baking soda
1 tsp. salt
1 small can crushed pineapple, drained
3 cups grated carrots
1 cup nuts, coarsely chopped

Blend oil and sugar until light and fluffy. Add eggs and beat until light. Sift dry ingredients and blend with egg mixture. Fold in pineapple, carrots and nuts. Place in 9x13-inch loaf pan. Bake at 350 degrees for 45-55 minutes.

Frosting

8 oz. cream cheese, softened
1/4 cup butter (margarine does not set as firmly)
1 pound powdered sugar
2 tsp. vanilla
1 cup slivered almonds, toasted

Blend and spread on cake. Decorate with toasted sliced almonds. Refrigerate after frosted.

Continued from page 39

FRUIT PIE

(Serves 8)

1 1/2 cups flour
1/2 cup corn oil
2 tsp. sugar
2 Tbsp. milk
1 tsp. salt
1/2 cup sliced almonds

Mix all ingredients together, except nuts, and press into 9-inch round pie pan. Prick with fork. Sprinkle sliced almonds on top. Bake at 375 degrees for 20 minutes. Cool.

Filling

1 8-oz. package cream cheese
1/2 cup sugar
1 tsp. vanilla

Mix ingredients together and spread onto cooled pastry. Decorate with assorted fruits: sliced strawberries, bananas, kiwis, cantaloupe, blueberries, raspberries

Glaze

1 cup orange juice
1/2 cup lemon juice
3/4 cup water
1 cup sugar
3 tsp. cornstarch

Cook ingredients until glaze thickens and turns clear. Spread over fruit and refrigerate.

WHITE SANGRIA

(Serves 8)

2 bottles (750 ml. each) dry white wine
1/4 cup Grand Marnier or brandy
1/4 cup superfine sugar

Continues on top of next page

10 strawberries, hulled and halved
1 navel orange, unpeeled and sliced
1 lemon, unpeeled and sliced
1 ripe pear, cored and sliced
1 peach, peeled, pitted and sliced
1/2 cup seedless grapes
2-3 cups chilled sparkling water
Ice
Mint sprigs, to garnish

Stir together wine, Grand Marnier and sugar in large pitcher. Add fruits, cover with plastic wrap and refrigerate 4-6 hours or overnight.

When ready to serve, add chilled sparkling water to taste. Serve over ice in large goblets and garnish with mint sprigs.

Continued from page 47

TACO SALAD

(Serves 12)

1 pound lowfat ground round beef
1/4 tsp. salt
1/2 tsp. garlic salt
1 15-oz. can drained kidney beans
1/2 cup green onions
4 tomatoes
1 head lettuce
2 large avocados
8 oz. Thousand Island dressing
4 oz. grated sharp Cheddar cheese
1 8-oz. bag taco-flavored corn chips, crushed

Season beef, then brown until no longer pink. Drain fat and add drained kidney beans. Mix and set aside. Chop onions, tomatoes, lettuce and avocados. Place in salad bowl and add beef and beans. Toss with Thousand Island dressing. Add Cheddar cheese and crushed corn chips. Toss again and serve.

NASTURTIUM BUTTER

(Makes 1 1/4 cups butter)

1/2 cup unsalted butter, at room temperature
1 cup nasturtium blossoms
2 Tbsp. nasturtium leaves, finely chopped
2 tsp. snipped chives

Cream butter until soft. Remove petals from the nasturtiums, saving one whole blossom. Slice and chop. Stir all ingredients gently into butter and mound attractively on serving plate. To garnish, place nasturtium blossom on top.

Continues from page 54

FRUIT CHUTNEY

(Makes 2 1/2 pints)

4 cups fruit (peaches, apples, pears, mangoes)
1 cup golden raisins, whole or diced
1 medium onion, finely chopped
2 cups sugar
1 1/4 tsp. ground ginger
2 cups water
2 cups apple cider vinegar
1/4 cup pickling spice (optional)

For a sharper flavor, cook with 1/4 cup pickling spice contained in a cheesecloth bag.

Combine all ingredients in 3- to 4-quart pan. Bring to a boil and simmer, uncovered, for 2 hours. Cool; remove cheesecloth bag, if used. Ready to serve. Will keep for weeks in refrigerator, indefinitely in freezer.

Recipes continue on page 88

Continued from page 87

MINT SLAW

(Serves 8)

4-8 oz. bacon, diced

1 medium head Napa cabbage

1 cup lightly packed mint leaves, chopped, or 1/4 cup dry flakes, crumbled

1/3 cup roasted peanuts

1/3 cup orange juice

3 Tbsp. white wine vinegar

1 1/2 tsp. sugar

Fry bacon until crisp. Drain on towel, leaving 3 Tbsp. drippings in skillet. Chop cabbage. Mix with mint, peanuts and bacon. Heat drippings and add orange juice, vinegar and sugar. Pour over cabbage.

BISCUIT BITS

(Serves 8)

1 8-oz. cylinder buttermilk biscuits

1/4 cup butter or margarine

1 1/2 tsp. dried parsley flakes

1/2 tsp. dill weed

1/4 tsp. dried minced onion or flakes

1 Tbsp. freshly grated Parmesan cheese

Melt butter in 10-inch round pan. Mix rest of ingredients, except biscuits, in the pan. Cut each biscuit in quarters, roll in butter mixture, put into pan so biscuits are touching and bake at 450 degrees for 8-10 minutes.

LICHEES IN CHAMPAGNE

Open can of lichees and drain. Place 4-6 lichees in the bottom of a champagne glass. Fill glasses with champagne and serve.

Continued from page 55

POPOVERS

(Makes 12)

2 cups flour

1/2 tsp. salt

5 eggs

2 cups milk

2 Tbsp. unsalted butter, melted

4 Tbsp. unsalted butter, cut into 12 even pieces

Preheat oven to 425 degrees and set rack in middle of oven. Oil popover or large muffin pans. Blend flour and salt and add eggs, milk and melted butter all at once. Mix with hand or electric mixer until batter has the consistency of heavy cream (1-2 minutes). Preheat popover pans in oven for 2 minutes. Place 1 piece of butter in each cup and return pan to oven until butter bubbles (about 1 minute). Fill hot pans half-full with batter and bake 20 minutes. Reduce heat to 350 degrees and bake 15-20 minutes more. Remove from oven and run knife around each popover. Remove from pan and serve.

Variations (add before mixing):

Orange: finely grated peel of 2 oranges

Dill-Shallot: 2 large shallots, peeled and finely minced, and 3 tsp. dried dill weed

Date-Walnut: 2/3 cup finely chopped dates and 1/2 cup finely chopped walnuts

Cranberry-Pecan: add 2 tsp. cinnamon, 1 tsp. ground ginger and 3 Tbsp. sugar to flour. Add 2/3 cup dried cranberries and 1/2 cup finely chopped pecans after milk.

Recipes continue on top of next page

Continued from page 88

FRESH LEMON ICE IN LEMON SHELLS

(Serves 6-8)

2 cups half-and-half (or heavy cream)
1 cup sugar
1-2 Tbsp. freshly grated lemon peel
1/3 cup freshly squeezed lemon juice
6-8 lemons, 1/4 top cut off, pulp and seeds removed

In large bowl, stir together half-and-half and sugar until sugar is thoroughly dissolved. Mix in lemon peel and juice. Pour directly into lemon shells. Freeze several hours until firm. Makes about 1 1/2 pints.

Continued from page 59

MARGARITAS

(Serves 8)

1 1/2 cups lime juice
1 1/2 cups tequila
1 cup orange-flavored liqueur
6 cups coarsely crushed ice
Salt-rimmed glasses
8 lime slices or wedges

Shake in a covered container, or whirl in a blender until slushy, the lime juice, tequila, liqueur and ice. Pour into glasses. If mixture is shaken, you can pour drink through a strainer and discard ice. Garnish with lime slices.

Continues from page 71

MICROWAVE FUDGE

(Makes 24 pieces)

1 pound powdered sugar
1/2 cup cocoa
1/4 cup milk
1/2 cup butter
1 tsp. vanilla
1/2 cup chopped nuts

Sift sugar and cocoa into glass bowl and blend well. Add milk and butter, but do not mix. Cook in microwave on High for 2-2 1/2 minutes. Remove from oven and stir. Mix in vanilla and nuts until blended. Pour into 8-inch square pan. Freeze 20 minutes or refrigerate 1 hour.

BROWNIES

2 squares (2 oz.) unsweetened chocolate
1 egg
1/4 cup butter or margarine, melted
1 1/4 cups dark brown sugar
1/2 cup flour
1/2 tsp. vanilla
1/2 cup walnuts, chopped
1/4 tsp. salt

Melt chocolate in top of double boiler over simmering water. Put remaining ingredients into large bowl and pour chocolate over. Mix. Turn mixture into greased 8-inch square shallow pan. Bake at 300 degrees for 30-40 minutes. Cut into squares.

Recipes continue on page 90

Continues from page 89

MINT SURPRISE COOKIES

(Makes about 6 dozen)

3 cups sifted flour
1 tsp. baking soda
1 tsp. salt
1 cup butter
1 cup sugar
1/2 cup brown sugar
2 eggs, unbeaten
2 Tbsp. water
1 tsp. vanilla
9-oz. package solid chocolate mint wafers
6 dozen walnut halves (optional)

Sift together flour, baking soda and salt. Cream together butter, sugar, and brown sugar. Add flour mixture. Mix. Blend in eggs, water and vanilla. Cover and refrigerate 2 hours. Enclose each wafer in 1 Tbsp. chilled dough. Place on greased cookie sheet 2 inches apart. Optional: Place walnut half on top of each cookie. Bake at 375 degrees 10-12 minutes.

Continued from page 75

ARTICHOKE ROUNDS

(Makes 24)

Artichoke hearts: 1 package frozen, or 1 can
24 toast rounds
1/4 cup butter, melted
1/4 tsp. garlic salt
Dash of pepper
3 Tbsp. Parmesan cheese

Cook artichoke hearts according to package directions (if using canned artichokes, do not cook). Drain well, cut-side down. Place each heart, cut-side up, on a toast round and put on baking sheet. Combine butter, garlic salt and pepper. Drizzle over artichokes. Sprinkle with Parmesan cheese. Let stand, covered, for up to 6 hours. Bake, uncovered, at 350 degrees for 10 minutes, or until thoroughly hot.

HEARTS OF PALM

(Serves 8)

1 8-oz. package sliced ham
8 oz. soft cream cheese
1 can hearts of palm

Spread cream cheese over ham slices. Place a heart of palm on ham slice and roll tightly. Slice in about 5 even pieces.

TRIFLE

(Serves 10)

Stale sponge cake
Ladyfingers (optional)
Raspberry jam or curd
Macaroons
1 cup sherry

Line the sides of glass bowl with ladyfingers. To see layers in bowl, omit this step. Cover the bottom of bowl with 1 1/2-inch layer of sponge cake. Spread a generous layer of raspberry jam or curd over the cake, and a layer of crumbled macaroons over the jam. Pour a cup of sherry over all, enough to saturate thoroughly. Put into refrigerator until needed.

Continues on top of next page

Continued from page 90

2 cups milk
6 egg yolks
1/2 cup sugar
Rind of 1/2 lemon, grated
1/2 tsp. salt
2 oz. brandy
1/2 tsp. vanilla

To make a boiled custard: Scald milk. Combine egg yolks with sugar, lemon rind and salt and beat lightly. Slowly add scalded milk to egg mixture and cook in double boiler, beating constantly, until thickened to coat a spoon. Add brandy and vanilla. Put into refrigerator to cool.

1/2 tsp. lemon extract
3 Tbsp. Chambord (raspberry liqueur)
2 Tbsp. dry white wine
2 cups heavy whipping cream
Sugar to taste
Quart fresh raspberries or strawberries
Slivered almonds

Mix lemon extract, Chambord, white wine, whipping cream and sugar to taste and whip until stiff. Place in refrigerator for several hours.

When ready to complete the trifle, place a layer of berries to cover the macaroon cake layer, cover with half the custard, a layer of half the whipped cream, a layer of macaroons, then layers of the remaining berries, custard, and whipped cream. Sprinkle slivered almonds on top.

Continued from page 83

MICROWAVE PEANUT BRITTLE

(Makes about 1 pound)

1 1/2 cups unsalted dry-roasted peanuts
1 cup sugar
1/2 cup light corn syrup
Pinch of salt
3 Tbsp. butter
2 tsp. vanilla
1 1/4 tsp. baking soda

Butter large baking sheet. In microwave-proof bowl, combine peanuts, sugar, corn syrup and salt. Microwave on High until mixture bubbles vigorously, about 6 minutes. Remove mixture from microwave and stir in butter and vanilla. Return to microwave and cook on High until candy turns light gold color, about 3 minutes. Remove bowl from microwave. Add baking soda to candy mixture and stir briskly (mixture will foam). Immediately pour onto buttered baking sheet. Pull brittle thin with two buttered forks. Let stand until cold and hard, about 30 minutes. Break brittle into pieces. Store in airtight container at room temperature for up to 1 month.

"I am a staunch believer in having one's cake and eating it, a principle I have followed greedily throughout my life."
Anne-Scott-James

Recipes continue on page 92

Continued from page 91

PECAN DIVINES

(Serves 16)

1/2 cup butter
1 1/2 cups flour
1/4 cup ice water
1 1/2 cups brown sugar
1 cup butter
1/2 cup honey
1/3 cup sugar
2 cups chopped pecans
1/4 cup whipping cream

Preheat oven to 350 degrees. Blend butter and flour until mixture resembles cornmeal. Add ice water and toss lightly. Roll in ball and chill for 1 hour. Roll dough into size to fit a floured, buttered 9x13-inch pan. Place in pan and prick with a fork. Bake 10 minutes. Remove from oven. Bring brown sugar, butter, honey and granulated sugar to a boil in heavy saucepan and boil until thick, stirring constantly, about 4 minutes. Remove from heat. Mix in pecans and cream. Pour over crust. Bake 25-30 minutes. Cool; cut into 3-inch diamonds or squares.

"One cannot think well, love well, sleep well, if one has not dined well."
    Virginia Woolf

LEMON COOKIE BARS

(Makes 25 bars)

<u>Base</u>

1 cup butter
1 cup sifted flour (measure before sifting)
1/4 cup powdered sugar

<u>Topping</u>

2 eggs
1 cup sugar
2+ Tbsp. flour
1/2 tsp. baking powder
1/3 cup lemon juice

Preheat oven to 350 degrees. Mix base together and pat into bottom of 8-inch square pan. Bake for 15 minutes. Beat eggs and sugar together. Add flour, baking powder and lemon juice. Mix. Spread topping over warm base. Bake 20 minutes (do not brown). Remove from oven and sprinkle with powdered sugar.

MINT TEA

(Serves 6)

4 tea bags of green tea
1 cup packed fresh mint leaves
1/4 cup sugar
3 cups boiling water

Place tea bags, fresh mint leaves and sugar in teapot. Pour 3 cups boiling water over and stir to dissolve sugar. Let steep 4 minutes and serve.

Acknowledgements

"LET'S DO LUNCH" COMMITTEE

NANCY BILDSOE	NANCY LAWTON	JERRIE SCHMIDT
KAREN BOWDEN	JOAN LIGHTNER	ILENE SWARTZ
BETTY BRAYSHAY	KARON LUCE	PAULA TAYLOR
PEGGY ELLIOTT	SANDRA MOOERS	JEAN THOMPSON
JOAN EVANGELOU	MARGE MYERS	GORDON THOMPSON
GEORG'ANN FLETCHER	CHARLENE RIGHTS	YOLANDA WALTHER-MEADE
GENE GAULT	MARY SADLER	B. J. WILLIAMS

Nancy Anderson
Emily & Michael Bagnall
Pat Beck
Keith Bennett
Mo Bildsoe
Alanna Bodenstab
Betty Brayshay
Cedar Hills Farm
Kathryn Crippen
Clark Crouse, Photography
Jean Davis
Alan Decker, Photography
Carol & Martin Dickinson
Barbara Donahue
Carolyn Elledge
Doris & Peter Ellsworth
Connie & Jerry Englert
Becki Etess
Joan Evangelou
Feather Acres Farm & Nursery
Jane Fetter
Jeanette Foushee
Libby Frank
Gene Gault
Dottie & Hal Georgens
Pat Gooding
André Grey

Lisa Hanly
Lynn Haynes
Nancy Herrington
Nancy Hewitt
Jody Honnen
Candace Kohl
Dick Laventhol
Jackie Leisz
Donna Losh
Karon & Gordon Luce
Barbara & Ed Malone
Katie Martin
Mary Ann McCauley
Barbara & Bill McColl
Diane Miller
Gladys Minchin
Ginny Misbach
Morgan Run
Janet Munson
Marjorie Myers
Sharon Neary
Marti & Frank Panarisi
Marianne & Douglas Pardee
Francis Perrot
Pioneer Centres
    Kerry Maguire
Kay Redmond
Charlene Rights

Pam Risher
Harold Sadler
San Diego Polo Club
Jerrie Schmidt
Shirley Schwab
Gretchen & Earl Schwensen
Barbara & Dick Sewall
Clarke Simm
Jane Smith
Jane & Jim Stockwell
Kay Stone
Sue & Steve Terris
Lois Thompson
Tiffany & Co., San Diego
    Mary Swanby
    Cathryn Ramirez
UCSD Graphics
Communications
    Edwin Dunn, Manager
    Aaron Borovoy
    Rick Stapa
Gloria & Bob Wallace
Marion & Tom Warburton
Mary Jane Wiesler
Wild Animal Park
Gayle Wilson
Elizabeth & Joe Yamada

Index

ENTRÉES

Achiote Chicken, 34
Brandied Veal, 22
Burgundy Beef, 30
Chicken Enchiladas, 58
Citrus-Balsamic Salmon, 50
Cornish Game Hens in Grand Marnier Sauce, 62
Crab Pizza, 66
Fish Stew with Rouille Sauce, 30
Garlic & Tarragon Chicken, 14
Honey-Mustard Pork, 38
Lamb Morocco, 30
Marinated Quail, 42
Meatloaf, 55
9-Boy Curry, 54
Pesto with Fresh Vegetables, 19
Sushi, 27

PASTA, RICE, BEANS, POTATOES

Fried Rice, 54
Mashed Potatoes, 55
Minted New Potatoes, 42
Orange Praline Yams, 39
Parslied Gnocci or Noodles, 22
Spicy Black Beans, 35
Tri-Color Pasta, 18
Wild Rice, 62

VEGETABLES

Asparagus Spears with Chives, 50
California Carrots, 55
Fennel Harvest, 31
Garlic Zucchini, 55
Miso-Marinated Asparagus, 27
Sautéed Portobello Mushrooms, 43
Vegetable Collage, 22

SAUCES

Fruit Chutney, 87
Mango & Passion Fruit Salsa, 35
Salsa, 59
Sambai-Zu Dipping Sauce, 26
Tomatillo Sauce, 58

DESSERTS

Baked Alaska, 71
Buñelas, 59
Cakes:
   California Cheesecake, 83
   Candy Kisses Cake, 79
   Carrot Cake, 86
   Chocolate Decorations for Cake, 70
   Ice Cream Cone Cakes, 78
   Lemon Cream Cake, 84
California Crêpes, 43
Candy:
   Candied Flowers, 79
   Microwave Fudge, 89
   Microwave Peanut Brittle, 91
   World's Finest Roca Candy, 83
Caramel Apple Crisp, 63
Chocolate Crème Brulée, 71
Chocolate Fondue, 70
Coffee Tortoni, 85
Cookies:
   Apricot Nut Bars, 67
   Biscuits de Noel, 83
   Brownies, 89
   Finger Cookies, 79
   Flower Cookies, 78
   Lemon Cookie Bars, 92
   Mint Surprise Cookies, 90
   Oatmeal Drops, 67
   Painted Cookies, 79
   Pecan Divines, 92
   Pralines, 66
Flan, 35
Fresh Lemon Ice in Lemon Shells, 89
Lichees in Champagne, 88
Orange Meringue Lovely, 23
Pies:
   Chocolate-Orange Pecan Pie, 70
   Date Meringue Pie, 15
   Fruit Pie, 86
   Macadamia Caramel Pie, 46
   Sour Cream Lemon Pie, 51
Sauces:
   Caramel Sauce, 63
   Guilt-Free Chocolate Sauce, 71
Tiramisu, 11
Trifle, 90-91